Marriage Story of Mary

Mary Yang is a youth and young adult preacher at All Nations Disciple Church and a translator at Sarang Jeil Church in Seoul, South Korea. In addition to church ministry, Mary is actively engaged in media ministry, appearing on online political talk shows and operating her own YouTube channel, heyMARY.

Mary was born in Los Angeles, California and raised in Grand Rapids, Michigan, in a pastor's family. Following her parents, Mary moved to Seoul, South Korea, in 2009, where she enrolled in Seoul Foreign School for her middle and high school years. In 2012, Mary enrolled in Emory University in Atlanta, Georgia, where she obtained her bachelor's degree in psychology and Chinese language and literature. Upon graduating, Mary remains a member of the Phi Beta Kappa Honor Society and Psi Chi International Honor Society in Psychology.

With a passion for missionary work, Mary and her husband, Enoch, co-founded Enoch and Mary Missions Organization in 2021. They currently have one child and make their home in Seoul, South Korea.

November 9, 2021

♥

*Dedicated to the Holy Spirit,
who ignited in me a love for writing His story.*

Recommendations

It is not an understatement to say that who you meet determines a lifetime, and among many relationships, that of a marriage is what most significantly determines your life's journey. Marriage can bring happiness, passion, and the achievement of goals that were once deemed impossible. But today, in getting married, many young adults rely on emotional feelings and personal judgment, only to find themselves in regret. The divorce rate in South Korea ranks third in the world, after the United States and the United Kingdom. This is a tragedy for South Korean society, a tragedy for future generations, and a tragedy for the country, and occurs due to mistakes in marital decisions. On the other hand, a successful marriage under God's guidance makes possible what once was impossible had one man and woman lived separate lives. A successful marriage under God's guidance can change the history of mankind and even determine the fate of an entire nation. The author of *Marriage Story of Mary*, after having understood the steps for a successful Biblical marriage, has detailed her living testimony in this book. I hope that *Marriage Story of Mary* will serve as a definitive guide to marriage for many young people in the future and that through this book, many successful marriages will occur once again in our society.

Pastor Jun Kwang-hoon (father-in-law)

Dear Mary,

I thank God for His having sent someone like you, who radiates love and joy to our family. I give God infinite thanksgiving for His having given us a precious treasure like you. And for you to have written a book that records your life's journey with Christ up to this marriage, I heartily congratulate you. Though it is impossible to convey my affection for you in these few words, I send you my infinite love from the bottom of my heart. Congratulations.

Seo Mi-young (mother-in-law)

Marriage Story of Mary tells the story of a young girl founding a Christ-centered marriage as she follows not the fading emotions of the world but the will of God. In October of last year [2021], upon returning home from a series of national prayer conventions in the United States under the leadership of Pastor Jun Kwang-hoon, the author began writing this book during her two-week traveler's quarantine. I am surprised at the author for even having taken the hiatus in her work as an opportunity to write a powerful book. I am confident that *Marriage Story of Mary* will be a valuable guide to Biblical marriage for hundreds of thousands of children and parents, bringing restoration to South Korea as a whole. All this glory, we give to God.

To my dear daughter Mary, you have always been a great joy to our family! Though there were difficult times in the early years of my studying abroad as a poor seminary student and ministering as a pastor, I was always able to overcome those times because of God's gift of you to me and your mother. Now, seeing the beautiful married life between you and Enoch as you nurture and love one another, I am overjoyed and well-assured. Seeing how you are dearly loved by your parents-in-law, who live by love and vision for Christ, I give thanks to God. Though I am far away in body, I still live each day with you in the Holy Spirit. As L. M. Montgomery of Anne of Green Gables records on the last page of her book, "God's in his heaven, all's right with the world." I hope that you remember this powerful confession for a lifetime. Congratulations, Mary!

Pastor Billy Yang (father)

If there is one thing that is most important to an individual, it is whom they meet. It is not an exaggeration to say that whom one meets determines an individual's life. However, there are encounters that one cannot choose, such as with our parents. This encounter is not a matter of choice but of the divine ordainment of God. And though most people deny it, there is another encounter that God has ordained in our lives: marriage.

Many young people today busily roam around in search of their "other half." However, *Marriage Story of Mary* records the true story of a girl following not her feelings and thoughts but only the voice of God in prayer to find her God-ordained other half.

I believe that this book, which is not a mere collection of tips and advice for marriage but rather the honest testimony of the author's journey, will have a profound influence on many young people as they prepare themselves for marriage.

I confidently believe that *Marriage Story of Mary* will shine to become a source of light and direction to a generation and country of broken values and broken marriages.

Pastor Sharon Yang (mother)

Table of Contents

Recommendations	6
Prologue: October's Bride	12
Chapter 01 My Story	20
Chapter 02 Mary, Can You Give Me Your Marriage?	27
Chapter 03 Death to Self	35
Chapter 04 Three Reasons Why It Was Difficult	40
Chapter 05 Giving Up My Emotions	56
Chapter 06 Mary, I Want to Give You More	63
Chapter 07 If It Is Your Will, I Will Marry Him	74
Chapter 08 Meeting Enoch	79
Chapter 09 Pastor Jun's Wedding Sermon: The New Jerusalem Wedding	85
Chapter 10 Where Is My Isaac?	90
Chapter 11 Who Is God to You?	97
Chapter 12 I Feel Comfortable When I'm Around You	106
Chapter 13 Mary's ⟨Future Husband⟩ Prayer List	112
Chapter 14 Two Qualities of a Beautiful Bride	127

Chapter 15 Parable of the Four Soils · 146

Chapter 16 Mary, I'm Sorry · 157

Chapter 17 Mary's Dream · 175

Chapter 18 Our Family's Dream · 201

Chapter 19 And, Mary's Last Dream · 207

Epilogue · 211

Prologue

October's Bride

On a breezy October day painted red and orange with crisp autumn leaves, I walked into the wedding hall for the moment I had waited for ever since I was a young girl. Under the flickering camera flashes and the jubilant cheers of family and friends, I took a moment to look at the big, warm hand that held steadfast to mine: The hand of a father, for 24 years, that had carried me from the moment I was born, had lifted me up from danger and death, and had pointed me to God in times of trouble and failure. Now, holding this hand as I walked down the wedding aisle, I realized that this hand had been not only that of my father but also that of God, who had always been with me.

Even before the beginning of life, God's hand had planned me, shaped me, carried me, protected me, and guided me to where I was today. And finally, 24 years later, on a beautiful October day, God's hand had led me to my beloved husband.

Ever since my mother first told me that marriage is important, when I was 13, I had prayed every day for my future spouse with a list of 30 items. But over time, God began to prove to me how far my ideal prayer list fell short of God's thoughts.

> "As the heavens are higher than the earth, so are my ways higher than your ways and my thoughts than your thoughts."
> (Isaiah 55:9)

What I wanted was to meet a man with a slim, fit body, of moderate height, with thickly framed glasses and a love for reading. What I had dreamed of was a natural encounter, perhaps at college, and after two years of dating, a small wedding with family and friends. But the plan of God, which led me to a 6'3 former high school football player to whom I was to commit my entire life in a single month, was beyond what I could comprehend.

The reason why I decided to marry this man was neither a moment's choice nor a fluttering emotion. The only reason I was able to obey God's will was because of the relationship with God that I had built over the preceding 24 years. It was this relationship that opened my eyes to see beyond my thoughts and emotions to recognize the most perfect companion that God had predestined for my life, and it was this relationship that ultimately brought to me the greatest blessing of marrying my husband at 24.

Marriage is not about meeting the person whom I deem most ideal but meeting the person whom God deems most ideal. In marital decisions, many young people today look at personality, family background, occupation, and other self-centered standards. Some individuals even choose to marry without any parental intervention. But if these individuals so trust their independent sense of judgment, why do so many of their marriages end in brokenness, failure, and divorce?

Today in South Korea, more than 300 married couples divorce each day. This ranks ninth among Organization for Economic Co-operation and Development (OECD) member countries and first in Asia. The decision that they had once been so confident about, in a few years, ends in regret. A marital judgment based on self-centered emotions, thoughts, and standards is clearly insufficient to recognize the most ideal spouse.

There is something young Christian men and women should remember. There is only one spouse whom God has prepared for us. And this spouse is the most ideal partner for us in God's eyes. Therefore, until the day that God leads us to this encounter, we need to equip ourselves not with our appearance and worldly standards but with open eyes, open ears, and an open heart to recognize the will of God.

Another thing to remember is that even a failed marriage, broken premarital chastity, and frustrated hopes for marriage can be restored in Jesus Christ. Have you given up on yourself due to a past divorce? Are you living in guilt due to a momentary wrong choice? Are your hopes of marriage crushed by low self-esteem and distrust of people? Even if you have been divorced, have lost premarital chastity, and have suffered through crushed hopes, there is no failure that can stand up against Jesus.

In the Bible, the majority of figures that represent our brideship to Jesus, including Judah's daughter-in-law Tamar, the prostitute Rahab, and the widow Ruth, were ethically and morally fallen people. This fallenness applies not only to those who have suffered through divorce, lost premarital chastity, and experienced crushed hopes but also to every one of us. Born with original sin, we are all unqualified to become brides of Jesus.

> "For all have sinned and fall short of the glory of God."
> (Romans 3:23)

However, the good news is that Jesus has given us a chance for restoration!

> "Therefore, if anyone is in Christ, the new creation has come: The old has gone, the new is here!"
> (2 Corinthians 5:17)

In Jesus, even a broken marriage, lost premarital chastity, and crushed self-esteem can be completely restored. I hope that *Marriage Story of Mary* becomes not a book of didactic knowledge but a book of God's love for you. I pray that *Marriage Story of Mary* does not stop at giving tips and advice for a successful marriage but goes beyond to touch your heart as God calls you to make new decisions in your walk with Him!

Sincerely,
Mary

This book is the story of how I prayed for ten years for my future husband.
This book is the story of how I married someone whom I met for the first time in a single month.
And this book is the story of how I met my eternal bridegroom, Jesus Christ.

This book is the Marriage *Story of Mary*.

Chapter 01
My Story

Born in California and raised in Michigan, I grew up as the daughter of a pastor of a small pioneering church. Preferring to play with friends than to study, being extremely shy in front of adults, and being scolded by my mother for stealing toys, I was a very ordinary child from an ordinary background and upbringing.

But the year 2009 brought a twist to my comfortable, ordinary life.

In 2009, my father finished his theological studies at Calvin Seminary in Grand Rapids, Michigan, and our entire family, which then consisted of me and my parents, packed our 11 years' worth of belongings to move to Seoul, South Korea.

Life in Korea was completely different from in America.

Learning to play the violin and piano, swimming, ice skating, dancing ballet, and taking picnic trips to the public library every weekend, America was a place of opportunities, comfort, and freedom. But life in Korea was completely different. Living in a two-roomed apartment with old, rusty water pipes, being scolded by the maintenance man every other month for overdue fees, and driving around in a used van covered with church stickers, I, for the first time, realized what poverty looked like, smelled like, and felt like.

It was then that I, for the first time in my life, decided to change my forever childhood dream of becoming a teacher. I realized that what I needed most was not a dream that would make me most happy but a dream that would make me the most money. *I needed to become a businesswoman.*

To achieve this goal, I gave myself to studying. Throughout my middle and high school years, I wholly committed my time, energy, hobbies, and interests to studying. Surely, hard work reaped academic achievement; however, this never-ending thirst for success gradually exhausted my mind and body. This thirst that could only be filled with the perfect love of God was something that I could not let go. Letting go of it meant letting go of the worth that people saw in me.

For the seven years of my middle and high school years, God always asked me the same question.

"Mary, will you let me be the Lord of your life?"

Looking back, my teenage years were a time of

responding to God's voice and obeying God's instruction to let go of my idols. Over the years, God worked in me, as a daughter of a poor pastor's family, to let go of my bondage to money and low self-esteem.

Obedience in letting go of what made me feel most secure and loved was not easy. Constant worshipping, praying, reading the Word of God, confessing sins, forgiving people, and obeying spiritual leaders were not easy. But the fruit of glory that such obedience bore was incomparable.

> "I consider that our present sufferings are not worth comparing with the glory that will be revealed in us."
> (Romans 8:18)

To me, that glory was freedom.

In worship, I began to know God. I began to realize that God was neither poor nor strict. God was a good Father who wanted to help me. As I got to know God, I began to feel the depths of His love through Jesus Christ, and this love began to revive my dying spirit. What a joy it became to worship every day, how exhilarating to pray, and how satisfying to read His Word! In the end, I was able to surrender my insecurities to the perfect Lordship of God. As an example, I began to give freely to God what I loved most—money—in the form of tithes, thanksgiving offerings, mission offerings, and relief offerings for those in need. After all, what could I not give to God when He had given me the greatest gift of Jesus Christ!

What freed me from the values and insecurities of the world was *worship*. True freedom comes when we obey the voice of God. And this freedom, which we enjoyed in the Garden of Eden, is the original self-image of mankind.

> "Now the Lord is the Spirit, and where the Spirit of the Lord is, there is freedom."
> (2 Corinthians 3:17)

As I committed myself to worship every day, God began to teach me how to pray, how to read the Bible, how to serve, and how to live for Jesus. It was then that I, while experiencing a level of mature faith, became satisfied with myself.

'There's nothing else that God will ask of me. I've already obeyed everything!'

But in the spring of 2021, to the 24-year-old who was content and convinced that she had given everything to God, God spoke again.

"Mary."

"Yes, God."

"What is that in your hands?"

"I have nothing in my hands. God, don't you know that I've already given you everything?"

"Mary."

"Yes?"

"What is that in your hands?"

(…)

"Can you give that to me?"

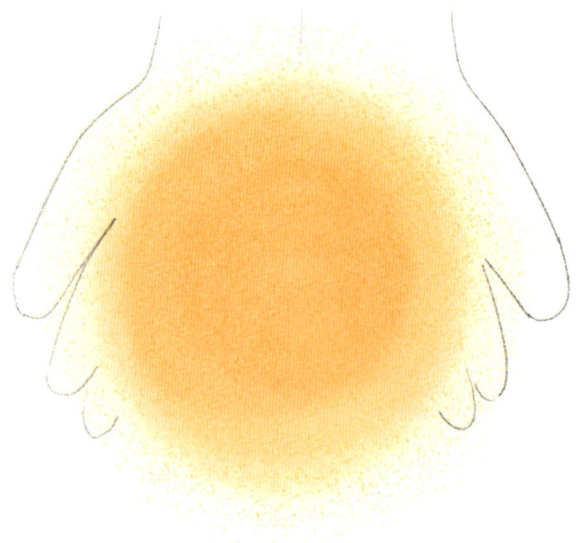

Chapter 02
Mary, Can You Give Me Your Marriage?

"Mary, can you give me your marriage?"

It was the third Sunday of March 2021 when God spoke to me. Serving as a translator every Sunday at Sarang Jeil Church in Seoul, South Korea, I would normally arrive at the church office by 10:20 AM and prepare myself for the 11:00 AM worship as I waited for the head pastor, Pastor Jun Kwang-hoon. But on that third Sunday of March 2021, I, for no special reason, arrived at 10:00 AM, one hour before worship, and Pastor Jun also happened to walk into the office 30 minutes earlier than usual.

"Good morning, pastor!"

"Good morning, Mary! How are you today?"

Ever since the first Sunday of August 2020, when I met Pastor Jun, he has remained a role model to me. Every Sunday as he walks into the church office with a slow yet firm walk, a bright and radiant smile, and waving hands, I see in him the Gospel of Jesus Christ. In him, I see the Gospel of suffering, death, and resurrection—the life of Jesus Christ. The life that Pastor Jun has lived is the kind of life that I admire, desire to imitate, and seek to surpass.

Like any other day, I welcomed Pastor Jun as he walked into the office.

"Pastor, how are you today?"

"Good, good."

Pastor Jun, who on any other day would immediately have started praying after seating himself, on that day, unexpectedly asked me a question.

"Mary."

"Yes, pastor?"

"Are you still dating your boyfriend?"

"No, pastor. We broke up in January."

"Oh, why did you not tell me?"

On August 9, 2020, my first Sunday translating at Sarang Jeil Church in preparation for the August 15th Gwanghwamun Rally the following week, Pastor Jun had asked me if I was dating anyone. At that time, having been in a relationship for three years, I had answered Pastor Jun that I was, and since then, he had never asked the question again. But surprisingly, over the succeeding six months, God, independent of Pastor Jun's question, convicted me of His will, and I obeyed by putting an end to the relationship.

After breaking up with my boyfriend, I no longer sought to commit myself to a relationship in the near future. And that was why I had not told anyone, except for family and close church friends, about my breakup.

"Oh, why did you not tell me?"

Smiling, Pastor Jun scolded me lightly.

"Mary, listen well. People give to God money and everything else, but in what is most important—marriage—they decide as they wish! They make a mistake in what matters most! Everything else is up to you, but when it comes to marriage, you have to listen to your spiritual leader and God."

The confidence that Pastor Jun spoke with was indeed justified.

Having obeyed the words of his spiritual leader to marry his wife, Pastor Jun had realized that this obedience in marriage was what made possible the big ministry he carries out today. But to me, this was never heard of. For me, marriage was meeting the person that God had prepared for me through *naturally occurring emotions*. What Pastor Jun said was utterly incomprehensible.

"When Enoch returns to Korea, go on a date!"

"Enoch?"

Enoch is the only son of Pastor Jun. Until then, I

thought that Enoch was the same age as I was, but regardless of his age, I had absolutely no interest in dating him. No matter what Pastor Jun said, I was determined to honor my decision.

'I've prayed for my future husband for ten whole years. I can't just date anyone.'

But every Sunday, regardless of my resolution, Pastor Jun mentioned Enoch.

"When Enoch returns from America in August, the two of you can go on dates and get married right away!"

"But pastor, feelings come first. We'll think about marriage if we do end up liking each other."

"No, no. There's nothing to think about. Feelings will naturally follow."

On Sundays, when there were guests in the pastor's office like the lawyers Kang Yeon-jae and Ko Young-il, Pastor Jun would talk about Enoch even more.

"It's marriage that one most needs to give to God!

Look at me! It's the fact that I married my wife that made this big ministry possible. Even if you obey God in everything, when you don't obey in what's most important, everything is in vain, isn't it?"

"That's right, pastor. It's important to heed our spiritual leaders when deciding who to marry."

"I'm trying to persuade Enoch and Mary, but these kids won't listen, ha-ha."

"Aw, Mary. You don't know how handsome and morally upright Enoch is! The last time I saw him bodyguarding Pastor Jun at the rallies, I was so touched."

The conversation between Lawyer Kang and Pastor Jun only made my heart grow heavier. It was then that I noticed Lawyer Ko nodding his head in agreement with their discussion.

A month prior, I had attended a conference for young Christian adults envisioning a legal profession and had been shocked at what Lawyer Ko had said during the last Q&A session on the topic of marriage.

"Because of your young age, you may not understand everything I am going to say. But remember this—marriage is 70% your parents' opinion, 20% the opinion of those around you, and only the remaining 10% is your own opinion."

At that time, the words of Lawyer Ko were a shock to me. And exactly one month later, seeing Lawyer Ko nod his head at Pastor Jun's words, I had an eerie feeling that this marriage might indeed be God's will.

As the days went by, every Sunday morning became a marriage counseling session, and with each week, my heart only grew heavier. This obedience was only possible if I surrendered my thoughts to God, and I knew that this death of my thoughts would be as painful as that of my body.

Chapter 03
Death to Self

In Genesis 3, Adam and Eve disobey God and eat from the Tree of the Knowledge of Good and Evil. As a result, they are not only expelled from the Garden of Eden but also lose spiritual communion with God. A loss of spiritual communion with God naturally induces a will that is *independent* of God's. This independent will is driven by a mind full of mental strongholds that seek to satisfy the sinful desires of the *self*.

According to 1 Thessalonians, God created man to consist of three components.

> "May God himself, the God of peace, sanctify you through and through. May your whole spirit, soul and body be kept blameless at the coming of our Lord Jesus Christ."
> (1 Thessalonians 5:23)

The *body* gives us a visible, physical form and allows feelings of thirst, hunger, and even sexual desire. It is a beautiful and healthy component of mankind. The *soul* is our sense of thought, emotion, and will. It is the free will of mankind. Finally, the *spirit* is what makes possible a relationship with the invisible God. It allows us to connect with, personally know, and interact with God, whom we cannot see with our physical eyes.

> "God is spirit, and his worshipers must worship in the Spirit and in truth."
> (John 4:24)

The only distinction between humans and animals is the presence or absence of the spirit. Animals, like humans, consist of a body and soul. The mother bird guards and cares for her young. But what the mother bird does not have is the spirit that makes possible a personal relationship with her Creator. Here, we recognize that the love of God toward mankind was special from the very beginning of creation. God created us in His image and has a desire to have fellowship with us as His children. God is personal to all mankind and is curious about how we feel and think.

But ever since the original sin that Adam and Eve committed at the Tree of the Knowledge of Good and Evil, every human is born with a will that is *independent* of God. Simply put, from the moment we are born, our thoughts, emotions, and will are in opposition to God's. We prefer the thoughts of Satan, enjoy the emotions of

Satan, and make the decisions of Satan. This is our *sinful nature*.

But even after being betrayed by His very own children, God chose *not* to give up on us.

> "And I will put enmity between you and the woman, and between your offspring and hers; he will crush your head, and you will strike his heel."
> (Genesis 3:15)

Immediately after Adam and Eve ate from the Tree of the Knowledge of Good and Evil, God promises His one and only begotten Son, Jesus Christ. God promises that whoever believes in Jesus as Lord and confesses with their mouth not only receives salvation but also experiences a resurrection in the *spirit*.

> "If you declare with your mouth, 'Jesus is Lord,' and believe in your heart that God raised him from the dead, you will be saved."
> (Romans 10:9)

The moment we receive Christ, our spirit is born again.

But what God then proceeds to ask of us is a series of *deaths*. These *deaths* are not of the physical, which has already been paid for by Jesus, but of the soul, which remains in the *old nature*, or *self*, that is under Satan's influence. It is this independent, unsurrendered, and rebellious *self* that God asks us to die to. These are a series of deaths to self as we obey God's call to worship, pray, praise, give offerings, renounce sin, and even trust His will in a God-ordained marriage. Only when we die to *self* by surrendering our independent thoughts, emotions, and will can we resurrect with Christ into a life that is full of the presence and glory of God, of rewards and blessings, and of supernatural power.

But this death to *self* is the most difficult kind of death because it is continuous and goes against everything that this world preaches.

Praying about the vision and ministry of Enoch's family, I had realized quite early on that Enoch was the one who God had chosen for me. But this death to self, surrendering my thoughts and emotions to God's will, was just as painful as taking my life, and I knew that I could not do it on my own.

Chapter 04
Three Reasons Why It Was Difficult

There were three reasons why it was difficult for me to surrender my independent thoughts, emotions, and will to God.

• Independent Thoughts

To me, marriage was the most precious thing in the world. Having carried a white envelope with a list of 30 prayers for my future husband in the back slot of my Bible ever since the sixth grade of middle school, I could not just marry *anyone*. Marrying just anyone seemed like disposing of my ten years of prayer. This was a mental stronghold, independent of God.

• Independent Will

Since middle school, I was known by my peers as a conservative Christian, perhaps too conservative, to the point where I would only hold hands with the boy I was going to marry. Marriage was something special to me, and casual flirting and dating were not valid options. Until my senior year of high school, I kept my resolution not to date any of the boys who liked me—until I met my ex-boyfriend.

Enrolling in college in America, I met my ex-boyfriend at a small Korean church in Georgia. He was the same age as I was, bright in personality, sociable and popular, and loved by the adults and friends around him. After being friends at church for a year, we naturally began dating during our sophomore year of college. Spending time with him was fun and exciting; it felt like having a lifelong best friend.

But dating someone who had not yet personally experienced God began to affect my faith. As someone like Peter in the New Testament, who had been so confident in my love for God, I soon found myself loving my boyfriend more than God. And as someone, like David in the Old Testament, who had found true satisfaction in God alone, I soon found myself trying to fill with the love of man what only the love of God could fill. As a result, my faith began to die. I became captivated with jealousy, worry, and lewd thoughts of sin. I began losing the dreams and passions that I once had, and the clear voice of God that had once given me purpose began to fade. To me, there seemed no way for restoration. I felt frustrated, hopeless, and lost.

It was during this time that God sent me to Pastor Per Ivar Winæss in Norway, Europe, for an encounter that was to become one of the greatest blessings of my life.

In the oak lodge cabins of the beautiful, green Norwegian highlands, Pastor Per led powerful worship every morning and evening in the presence of the Holy Spirit. My boyfriend, who had followed me on the mission trip, would leave the service halfway to fiddle with his phone, saying that the worship was too long. But unlike him, with each day of worship, I began to feel my dying spirit coming back to life. New tongues and spiritual songs broke out, and God's voice began to resonate ever more clearly. Standing before the full presence of God in worship, tears of repentance began to fall, and slowly, God began to regain His Lordship over my humbled heart.

Returning from the mission trip that had begun a revival in me, I did not want to again lose the joy, peace, and freedom that I had experienced in worship. For the remaining two months of my summer break, I continued a daily lifestyle of worshipping, reading the Bible, and praying. And returning to America to complete my senior year of college, I strenuously maintained a life of worship, praying for an hour every morning and evening. This restoration of worship brought powerful changes to my life. Worship put an end to the sins that I had struggled with, worship reordered God as my first priority, and worship opened my eyes to see what I could not see in the past.

As my spiritual relationship with God was restored through worship, I began to see people in a different way. The Holy Spirit revealed to me that my boyfriend, whom I loved so dearly, had no burning desire to know God. He showed me that no matter how hard I tried to force him to pray and read God's Word, this desire was something that I could not give. So, for the last year and a half of our dating relationship, God trained me to let go. Like Abraham's obedience to God in sacrificing his one and only son, Isaac, on Mount Moriah, the last year and a half was a time of the most painful obedience in my life.

"God! There is nothing impossible for You! Why can't You change him, as I ask? Why can't You just force in him a heart like mine so that we can do Your Kingdom's work together!"

Putting an end to all my efforts in trying to build my boyfriend's faith was like Abraham's offering of Isaac on the altar. Putting an end to all my efforts and solely waiting for my boyfriend himself to seek God were acknowledging the painful possibility that God might take this person, whom I loved the most, away from me. Trusting in God's sovereignty over what I loved most was not an easy thing to do. But what we need to remember is this: In worship, where the presence of the Holy Spirit dwells, God fills us with His love by which we build our trust in Him. For six months, I surrendered my thoughts, emotions, and will to God. For six months, I focused my heart on worship and prayer. And six months is what it took me to completely give what I loved most into the perfect hands of God. Whether this relationship ended in marriage or a breakup, I had chosen to follow God's will.

In the end, my boyfriend and I broke up after three years of dating. Some may say that our relationship, having ended in a breakup, was a failure. But God says otherwise. Looking back, this relationship not only equipped me as a worshiper but also powerfully changed my boyfriend. Immediately after breaking up, he began, for the first time in his life, to shed tears of repentance and seek God. During such a time of brokenness, there was no one that he could hold onto except for God. It was during this time of complete drought in his life that he encountered Jesus as the only source of living water and was re-convicted of His love. Today, he is actively serving in the young adults' ministry of a large Korean church in Georgia and envisions becoming a preacher of God's Word. Hallelujah! This breakup that people had viewed as heartbreaking, to God, was life's most precious opportunity for the greatest encounter.

Many young adults in the church ask me about dating. As a topic of great interest to many young Christian adults, dating entails many questions, such as when to start dating, what type of person to meet, the healthy boundaries of physical touch, and many more. To answer such questions, there exist hundreds and thousands of Christian books. But what I have realized through my journey is that the absolute requirement for healthy Christian dating is *worship*. To foster a healthy, God-centered relationship, I, myself, need to first become a *worshiper*.

But do the young adults of today's generation think the same? Unfortunately, no.

"Worship is boring."

"I'd rather spend time doing something more efficient than worshiping."

To such a generation, I confidently say that the only reason that worship seems boring is because there has not yet been a genuine experience of what true worship is in their lives.

> "Yet a time is coming and has now come when the true worshipers will worship the Father in the Spirit and in truth, for they are the kind of worshipers the Father seeks."
> (John 4:23)

True worship is filled with the presence of the Holy Spirit. Worship makes us realize our sins and gives us strength to overcome them. Worship comforts the brokenhearted and reveals the will of God. Finally, worship teaches us the Word of God by which we evaluate and guide ourselves.

> "For the Word of God is alive and active. Sharper than any double-edged sword, it penetrates even to dividing soul and spirit, joints and marrow; it judges the thoughts and attitudes of the heart."
> (Hebrews 4:12)

In worship, there is a restoration that only the Holy Spirit can give.

> "The Spirit of the Sovereign LORD is on me because the LORD has anointed me to proclaim good news to the poor. He has sent me to bind up the brokenhearted, to proclaim freedom for the captives and release from darkness for the prisoners."
> (Isaiah 61:1)

In worship, the poor receive good news, the

brokenhearted are healed, and the captives are set free. In worship, there is complete restoration in our relationship with God. Without such restoration, we cannot manage or nurture any individual or organization according to God's will. The same principle applies ever more to dating. If we begin dating someone in the absence of an active, personal relationship with God, that romantic relationship is sure to draw us away from God—not closer. If we begin dating someone in the absence of an intimate relationship with God, that romantic relationship is sure to induce the negative emotions of jealousy, lewd thoughts, sins, worries, and anxieties. If we begin dating someone in the absence of a daily lifestyle of worship and prayer, that romantic relationship is sure to lead us away from the vision that God calls us to. These words are true and reliable.

For those that do not yet have any dating experience, do not be anxious. Having much dating experience does not necessarily mean success in marriage. If our ultimate goal is success in marriage, we need to turn our attention to God, who is the Governor of all encounters in a lifetime. It is only God who currently knows the name, age, family background, hobbies, interests, and even the God-ordained dreams of and plans for our future spouse. All encounters begin in the hands of the sovereign God. Therefore, whether in marriage or business, we must learn to entrust all that we seek to God, by faith.

> "Commit to the LORD whatever you do, and he will establish your plans."
> (Proverbs 16:3)

For those that are undergoing a relationship that is falling apart, do not be anxious. Have you become distant from God? Has your life of worship and prayer become your last priority? Are you committing sin and compromising your holiness? Are your God-given dreams fading away? If you are feeling as such, that is the Holy Spirit speaking to you through your conscience. Even now, the Holy Spirit is calling you to a place of worship and seeking to give you complete restoration. Worship is a place of the powerful presence of the Holy Spirit. The more we dwell in worship, the more the Holy Spirit can reveal God's thoughts to us. As the Holy Spirit pierces our conscience and gives rise to certain emotions, we must train to be sensitive and responsive to the work of the Holy Spirit in us. If we refuse to listen to and obey the help of the Holy Spirit, we are bound to be trapped in an endless cycle of sin.

> "For the wages of sin is death, but the gift of God is eternal life in Christ Jesus our Lord."
> (Romans 6:23)

From the moment we lose God as our first priority, we commit all kinds of sins, such as those of low self-esteem, anxiety, jealousy, worry, theft, murder, and sexual immorality. And because the same applies to dating, God often uses breakups to rescue those who are unresponsive to Him. Though many think that breakups occur because of each other's shortcomings, these breakups also occur because they have been permitted by God. Why does God permit them? *In order to deliver us.*

Is there any way to overcome the pain involved in breakups? Surely there is: *to love God more than anyone else.* When God becomes your number one priority, regardless of whether the dating relationship ends in marriage or a breakup, both sides acknowledge God's will and support each other's paths without being hurt. In a God-centered relationship, in which both sides' first priority is God, there is holiness, personal growth, and above all, faith that God will bring out His goodness in all circumstances. The following illustration, which God revealed to me in the summer of 2019, is the principle of what a God-centered dating relationship looks like. This is what you and the person whom you love must resemble.

"And we know that in all things God works for the good of those who love him, who have been called according to his purpose."
(Romans 8:28)

Remember this: There is only one spouse that God has prepared for you from the beginning of time. Therefore, experiencing a breakup does not mean that you have failed to meet the standards of the one you love but rather means that God is calling you back to the place where you belong, the place He has planned for you, the place where His faithfulness abounds. To overcome any remaining sorrows of a past breakup, you need to believe in the goodness of God.

Three weeks after I broke up with my boyfriend, I got a text message from him.

"Mary, in the process of our breakup, I realized that over the past three years of dating, I had loved you more than God. Honestly, this breakup wasn't easy for me at all. But when I think about it now, this breakup is what helped me seek and meet God. And now, I'm so thankful."

Through the breakup, God had gifted him the greatest encounter, an encounter with Jesus, which surpasses any relationship of mankind. Who is Jesus? Jesus is the Creator God Who knows us best. Meeting Jesus is the best encounter of a lifetime. Meeting Jesus is like a hidden treasure for which we would give all that we have to buy.

> "The Kingdom of heaven is like treasure hidden in a field. When a man found it, he hid it again, and then in his joy went and sold all he had and bought that field."
> (Matthew 13:44)

There were several reasons why I chose to end my three years of dating. But the most important reason was the longing for the Kingdom of God inside of me. After graduating from college, my dream was to eventually return to South Korea to pursue my vision of world missions while my boyfriend's dream was to remain in America to get married, have children, and pursue a comfortable and ordinary life. Of course, it was not that I did not want to have a family of my own. But for me, life could not be just that. To me, there was a greater purpose in the life that God had given me, and losing this purpose felt like dying. That is why, even forsaking the relationship, I could not lose what gave me the greatest meaning in life. Looking back, this was not personal ambition or desire but, instead, a calling of the Holy Spirit.

After breaking up with my boyfriend, I determined for myself:

'From now on, I'm only going to meet someone who can share my passion and vision for God. Before dating, I'm going to make sure that he's ready. I'm going to make sure that he reads the Bible on his own, prays on his own, and has an active relationship with God without my help.'

I was determined to keep this resolution and was more confident than ever that I would keep this promise. But it was after only a little while that I found myself wavering.

A new person had appeared before me.

Chapter 05
Giving Up My Emotions

After breaking up with my boyfriend, someone new appeared before me. This was the last and most significant reason why it was difficult to accept God's will.

• Independent Emotions

The new person who appeared in front of me had everything my ex-boyfriend lacked. He read the Bible on his own and prayed daily. When I would share my passion for God, he would share the same excitement and enthusiasm, and when I would talk about my vision for God, he would join in helping me achieve that vision. It was the first time that I had ever met someone who was so similar in personality, conversational code, and, of course, passion for God. Though I had not yet considered dating, I thought perhaps this person was to become my future spouse.

Naturally, as we began spending more time together, we grew closer and closer. And one day, when that person had the courage to confess his feelings for me, I found myself wishing for him to become my future spouse.

When I realized that I, too, had begun to have feelings for him, I immediately shared this with my mother. As a personal rule that I had kept ever since I was a child, sharing everything about my life with my mother, no matter how embarrassing or shameful, had helped to direct me on the right paths during critical moments of my life. What made this relationship possible was that I viewed my mother not only as a parent but also as a spiritual leader. And my mother, in response, had always guided me with compassion and wisdom. To me, my mother was a *little Jesus*.

That day, as usual, I told my mother everything. I shared with her why I liked him, why he was a potential spouse, and why he was the one to perhaps share my dreams for a lifetime. But my mother's reaction was completely different from what I had expected.

"I don't think so."

"What do you mean?"

"I don't think he's the one for you. Let's pray more and ask God."

As a daughter who had always obeyed immediately, I, for the first time ever, felt like my mother might be wrong. My will, independent of God, did not want to heed to God's Word speaking through my mother.

But God did not give up on me.

> "Being confident of this, that he who began a good work in you will carry it on to completion until the day of Christ Jesus."
> (Philippians 1:6)

Through my ministry of preaching, God began to awaken an awareness of my independent will. Though I felt an indescribable joy while preaching, as soon as I stepped down from the pulpit, I began to feel anxious.

'The only reason there was power in my preaching today is because of the Holy Spirit. If I pursue what is not God's will, the power of the Holy Spirit cannot remain in me. Even if the Holy Spirit desires, He cannot work in me. I feel so much joy preaching God's Word, but if I continue in disobedience, I will lose God's supernatural power inside of me.'

In the end, what rescued me was the ministry that God had given me. Through preaching, I began to grow aware of my independent will, and it was at Sarang Jeil Church's 11:00 AM Sunday service that this awareness grew most acute.

Serving as a translator for Sarang Jeil Church's Sunday service, I realized that there is something special about translating God's Word. When translating worldly knowledge, skill and experience can suffice. But when translating God's Word, which is inspired by the Holy Spirit, it is not human skill but the indwelling presence of the Holy Spirit that builds a powerful worship. Then, to whom does the Holy Spirit appear? It is to those who have completely surrendered to God. Complete surrender to God brings the complete presence of the Holy Spirit.

> "We always carry around, in our body, the death of Jesus, so that the life of Jesus may also be revealed in our body."
>
> (2 Corinthians 4:10)

Sarang Jeil Church's Sunday service begins with a praise medley in the following order.

두 손 들고 찬양합니다
(I Lift My Hands to the Coming King)

아버지 사랑합니다
(Father, I Love You)

성령이여 우리게
(Holy Spirit, to Us)

나 주님의 기쁨 되기 원하네
(To Be Pleasing You)

내 마음에 주를 향한 사랑이
(The Way of the Cross, the Life of the Martyr)

Translating Pastor Jun's Sunday sermon for a whole two hours, I had no choice but to always seek the help of the Holy Spirit. Without the help of the Holy Spirit, I could neither physically nor mentally endure, and it was this praise medley that gave me the perfect time to pray.

"Father God, You already know that I stand on this pulpit because I love You! So, please help me. Without Your help, I cannot do anything. Please take full charge of me today."

Every time I prayed like this, God answered me with a gentle, inner voice.

"Mary, I will never take my Spirit away from you. So, be free!"

But God, who had always planted in me words of promise and encouragement, from a certain moment, began pointing out something that was more important to Him than any powerful translating.

My independent will.

Chapter 06
Mary, I Want to Give You More

"Mary."

"Yes, God?"

"I want to give you more."

I knew exactly what God was implying. Refusing to respond to the direction that the Holy Spirit was giving me and rather following my independent will, I had begun to experience great difficulty in translating. I no longer felt like I was speaking with the fire of the Holy Spirit but, instead, merely assembling words to match each sentence. The dying of my once living and active translating left me with sharp pain and sorrow. This sorrow was not because I had lost the power of God inside of me but because I realized, for the first time, how I loved my independent will more than God.

The Holy Spirit knows and conducts the will of God. So, the moment I chose to follow my independent will by continuing my romantic feelings for the new person who had appeared before me, I had refused the Holy Spirit who was working inside of me.

> "And He who searches our hearts knows the mind of the Spirit because the Spirit intercedes for God's people in accordance with the will of God."
> (Romans 8:27)

The Holy Spirit loves and fulfills the will of God. Fulfilling the will of God is the very driving force behind and reason for the Holy Spirit's work and power. That is why for those who do not obey God's will, the Holy Spirit has no choice but to withdraw His power.

At age 24, I had already personally encountered the Holy Spirit. I was aware that it was the Holy Spirit, not my human skill, who cultivated in me talents and giftings in which He, Himself, delighted the most. But in the face of my continual disobedience, the Holy Spirit had no choice but to withdraw His power from me. And it was on that pulpit in that Sunday service that the Holy Spirit touched my conscience to recognize His sorrow toward my disobedience. In realizing the lamentation of the One who loves me most yet seeing myself still obstinate and unchanging, my heart ached to the point of death.

But the very pain that I felt on that pulpit was the beginning of my return to God. It was that very pain that gave me a reason why I needed to surrender my independent will to the perfect will of God. I loved God more than anything in this world, and that was exactly why I had to surrender.

For the death of *self* to take place, we need the baptism of love. In the Bible, there are many types of baptisms: baptism with water, baptism with fire, and baptism of the Holy Spirit. But there is also the baptism of love.

Without the baptism of God's love, we cannot overcome selfishness and self-victimization. It is only when we are filled with and restored by the love of God that we can empty ourselves, empty our old nature, and empty our sinful desires to allow the will of God to flow freely in our lives.

This baptism of love does not stop at only giving personal restoration. It goes beyond to ignite in us a Christ-like love for the lost souls around us.

Every Sunday, when I translate, I see hundreds of saints sitting before me. Driving from all across the country, these saints come hours early to prepare for the Sunday service that they have waited an entire week for. When the pastor preaches, the saints, glowing in holy desire for God's Word, never take their eyes off him. It was to these saints that the Holy Spirit, one day, directed my attention.

"Look! These are the souls you are to serve. Aren't they beautiful?"

"Yes, God, they are!"

"But, Mary?"

"Yes, God?"

"How many more souls like these?"

The Holy Spirit struck a painful blow to my conscience. Even when God had bestowed on me the ministry that I called my greatest passion, I was destroying this calling by chasing after someone who was not God's will for me. It was this passion for ministry, along with my love for God, that made my independent will no longer bearable.

> "Jesus replied: 'Love the Lord your God with all your heart and with all your soul and with all your mind.' This is the first and greatest commandment. And the second is like it: 'Love your neighbor as yourself.'"
>
> (Matthew 22:37–39)

Amidst my conflicted thoughts and emotions, the one thing that I did was continue worshiping and praying daily. In daily worship and prayer, the baptism of love began to pour into me a love for God and a love for lost souls more than I had ever experienced in the past. The only way to overcome every and any problem is to *remain* in worship. Do not give up on pushing yourself to a place of worship daily. This is the most powerful secret to surrendering your independent will and shortening your time in the wilderness. We need to remember that we cannot find any solution inside of us. It is in the Holy Spirit who works in our time of worship, time of reading God's Word, and time of prayer that we can find the most perfect and complete solution. Therefore, we need to give more time to the Holy Spirit: more time to speak to us, more time to reveal to us, and more time to work in us. It is only worship that illuminates and gives strength to the voice of the Holy Spirit that helps us to obey the will of God.

Like this, the Holy Spirit began to work busily inside of me. The Holy Spirit shared and enlightened my spirit to love God and the lost souls around me ever more than before. The Holy Spirit comforted me, encouraged me, and showed me how much He loved me. Our spiritual fuel is the love of God.

> "No, in all these things, we are more than conquerors through him who loved us."
>
> (Romans 8:37)

In the end, it was the baptism of God's love that gave me the strength to let go of my independent will. The process took several months, and it was not easy. I complained to, yelled at, and resented God. Countless times did I say hurtful things to God that I should not have said.

"God, why me? Why do you only do this to me? Just because I have a big vision for You doesn't mean you have to do this to me!"

But just like my mother had always taught me ever since I was young, I remained in worship, and in worship, I began to find strength in God.

When I had gained enough strength, the Holy Spirit immediately spoke to me.

"I want you to tell him today."

To whom does the Holy Spirit speak? To those who obey. That is why obedience is what is most important in the Christian life.

"But Samuel replied: 'Does the LORD delight in burnt

offerings and sacrifices as much as in obeying the LORD? To obey is better than sacrifice, and to heed is better than the fat of rams.'"

(1 Samuel 15:22)

Immediately, I obeyed. On the day that the Holy Spirit spoke to me, I made it clear to the person that this relationship was not God's will and that God had someone else, more complete in God's eyes, planned for both of us. This, of course, was not easy for him to accept or understand. He was indignant and resentful.

"How can you so suddenly get rid of your emotions and move on? Are you even human?!"

Listening to his hurtful words, I could not say a single thing. Everything he had said was true. It was me who chose to like him, and it was me who chose to cut him off. It was then that I realized again that I was a *sinner.* At that moment, I realized that there was absolutely no good inside of me and that the only thing I could do was to pray to God, the perfect problem solver in all situations.

'God, this is how terrible of a person I am. I've been a terrible person to him and to You. I'm a sinner who isn't capable of solving anything in my life. All I can do is to depend on You. Please help him understand Your good will in the same way that I have. Please comfort his broken heart and help him to be used greatly for Your Kingdom's work.'

> "I have been crucified with Christ, and I no longer live, but Christ lives in me. The life I now live in the body, I live by faith in the Son of God, who loved me and gave himself for me."
>
> (Galatians 2:20)

This was a complete surrender to the will of God. It was not for my own benefit that I had died to *self*. And it was not for Enoch, whom I would meet months later, that I had died to *self*. The reason I had surrendered my emotions was because of my love for the will of God and, surprisingly, because of what God had shown me about this person that I needed to cut off.

While in the midst of getting rid of my emotions, my mother shared with me a dream that she had one night.

"Mary, I don't know how you're dealing with your feelings for that person right now, but today I had a dream about him."

"What dream?"

"That person was trying to fly in the sky, but because of the thin thread that was tying him down to you, he couldn't. God told me that for him to fly, it was you who had to cut the thread."

The moment I realized the meaning of this dream, that this soul would not be able to achieve God's vision because of me, I was given a clear conscience to sever the last remaining emotional bond that I had been holding onto. To me, as someone who delights the most when seeing people fulfill God's vision, God had spoken in the most powerful way through my mother.

With that final revelation, I completely returned my independent will back to the faithful hands of God. And in relief over a long-fought battle, I could only shed tears of gratitude and joy. It was then that I, again, made a firm resolution, stronger than ever before.

'I'm not going to like anyone for the next few years. Now, I really want to just spend time with God and God alone!'

But God thought differently.

Chapter 07
If It Is Your Will, I Will Marry Him

The two people who influenced me the most in surrendering my independent will to God were my mother and Pastor Jun.

Throughout the time during which I had broken up with my ex-boyfriend and dealt with my emotions for the new person who had appeared before me, I had never told Pastor Jun. But while I was struggling the most to give up my emotions, Pastor Jun preached for two weeks about the Tree of the Knowledge of Good and Evil in Genesis 3. He preached that because of the original sin of Adam and Eve, all mankind is born with thoughts, emotions, and a sense of will *independent* of God, which must be surrendered to restore full communion with God.

While translating Pastor Jun's preaching, I was shocked. Through Pastor Jun, God was teaching me something that I had never known about myself.

"That's right! The reason that I'm struggling right now is because my thoughts, emotions, and will are independent of God!"

Through Pastor Jun's sermon, I realized for the first time that the cause of this struggle was my independent will. God's Word gave me enlightenment, and this enlightenment brought powerful changes to my life.

> "All Scripture is God-breathed and is useful for teaching, rebuking, correcting and training in righteousness, so that the servant of God may be thoroughly equipped for every good work."
>
> (2 Timothy 3:16-17)

From that time on, the name *Enoch*, which had once been a burden to accept, began to resonate in my heart. But this resonance was not yet one of pure joy but one of sadness.

One Sunday night in July of 2021, two weeks after

having completely surrendered my will to accept God's, I locked my bedroom door and knelt on my bed to pray to God.

"God, to be honest, I'm afraid. He's someone that I've never met, and I don't know a single thing about what he's like. We may not even end up liking each other. But God, if it is your will, I will marry him."

To me, this confession to accept God's will was like the confession of Jesus at Gethsemane. It was a confession that even though I may not end up being loved by my husband for the rest of my life, I would choose to marry him—because I loved God. That night, I cried for an hour before falling asleep.

> "'Abba, Father,' he said, 'everything is possible for you. Take this cup from me. Yet not what I will, but what you will.'"
> (Mark 14:36)

Though overjoyed that I had surrendered my independent will, I found myself sad and bitter toward God. One evening after a weekday church service, I prayed to God frankly.

"God, do you know how much I love you?"

"Of course, I do."

"Then why do you ask so much of me?"

(…)

"I see my friends naturally choose who to date and who to marry, but don't they live happily? You know that marriage is the most important thing to me, but why? Why only me?"

Kneeling in prayer, I desperately sought God for an answer. *Why? Why only me?* As I was repeating this question, I began to feel a sudden warmth surging up inside of me. Tears welled up in my eyes as God answered my question in a way that was to change my life forever.

"Because it's important to you."

The reason God required this obedience and intervened in my marriage was because what was most precious to me was also most precious to God. What his daughter most valued, Father God equally valued. The realization of the faithfulness of God's love turned all my remaining sorrow to shouts of praise.

> "And provide for those who grieve in Zion—to bestow on them a crown of beauty instead of ashes, the oil of joy instead of mourning, and a garment of praise instead of a spirit of despair. They will be called oaks of righteousness, a planting of the LORD for the display of his splendor."
> (Isaiah 61:3)

Chapter 08
Meeting Enoch

Canaan was a land that was conquered solely by faith in God's Word. When Joshua and the Israelites conquered Canaan, the first piece of land they had to fight for was the city of Jericho. To me, the journey to marry Enoch was like marching around the heavy walls of Jericho.

"See, the LORD your God has given you the land. Go up and take possession of it as the LORD, the God of your ancestors, told you. Do not be afraid; do not be discouraged."
(Deuteronomy 1:21)

The first day I met Enoch was August 26, 2021. Wearing a beige T-shirt, black pants, and black slippers, Enoch looked not like one typically would on a first date but like one typically would on a late-night run to the supermarket.

'If Enoch was interested in me, he would have dressed up more. He really doesn't seem to have any feelings for me.'

Glancing at the 6'3 bulky giant before me, I thought how different Enoch was from my ideal type of guy.

'Will I ever be able to grow feelings for Enoch?'

In beginning a relationship with Enoch, I needed two kinds of faith. First, I needed faith that Enoch, who had no interest in me, would eventually develop romantic feelings for me. Second, I needed faith that I, who had a solid set of ideal standards for physical appearance and personality, would end up liking Enoch.

> "Now faith is confidence in what we hope for and assurance about what we do not see."
>
> (Hebrews 11:1)

Every day and night, I began praying to the Holy Spirit.

"Holy Spirit, please help me. Let me like Enoch, and let Enoch like me too."

But contrary to what I expected, the Holy Spirit began to maximize my faith. Whenever I met Enoch, the Holy Spirit drew my attention not to whether Enoch had feelings for me but to what was more important to the Holy Spirit—*getting to know Enoch*. Listening to his joys, struggles, and life story, I found myself no longer worried and anxious. Instead, what began to take hold in me was a holy confidence that God had no option but to help me, who was following His will in all that I sought—even the heart of Enoch.

> "And without faith, it is impossible to please God because anyone who comes to him must believe that he exists and that he rewards those who earnestly seek him."
>
> (Hebrews 11:6)

During our third date, my faith began to manifest itself in action. After the date was over, while we were talking in my car before parting ways, the Holy Spirit suddenly began stirring my heart.

"Mary, just be yourself!"

"Be myself?"

I knew, of course, what the Holy Spirit was implying. After being in silence for a couple of seconds, I looked Enoch straight in the eyes. Fixing my eyes on Enoch's, I felt, in my heart, a small flutter. Enoch, blushing, turned his shaky eyes away from me. This time, reaching for his cheeks with both hands, I held onto his face and looked closer into Enoch's now-widened eyes.

"Enoch."

"… Yeah?"

"One day, you're going to end up liking me!"

That night, driving back home, I cried and cried. It was not because I immensely loved Enoch that I confessed my feelings for him but because I loved God that I actively chose to do so. Having to confess my feelings for this man who absolutely had no feelings for me made me feel sad, shameful, and lonely. But in such a moment of sorrow and deep loneliness, Jesus came to me. Crying in my car, I wiped my tears to heed to the voice of Jesus, who, through the Holy Spirit, was speaking to me.

"Mary, I love you."

Tears began to flow down my cheeks. Jesus was telling me that just as I was unidirectionally loving

Enoch and confessing my affection for him, He had loved me unidirectionally all along. The perfect Jesus never stopped loving someone as unfaithful, sinful, and disobedient as me! It was on this loneliest day of my life that I most deeply experienced the love of Jesus. To have someone love me like Jesus, driving back home on the highway, I yelled at the top of my lungs!

"Jesus! You are my eternal bridegroom, and I am your bride!"

Through the process of meeting my husband, I met my eternal husband, Jesus Christ. This encounter with Jesus completely changed my focus in life. Though I was to get married, my eternal bridegroom was Jesus, and the greatest wedding banquet of my life was to be the Second Coming of Jesus. In all the work and studies that I would engage in for a lifetime, I would live not for personal glory but for the glory of my bridegroom, Jesus. And through all the persecution in following in the footsteps of Christ, I could endure, persevere, and overcome in His love. Now, nothing was impossible for me. The life of Heaven down on earth, the life of *New Jerusalem*, had begun.

Chapter 09
Pastor Jun's Wedding Sermon
: The New Jerusalem Wedding

Every human marries twice. The first marriage is the physical marriage between one man and one woman. The second marriage is the marriage of the Christian believer to Jesus, as written in Revelations 21. Though many people seek success only in the physical marriage, God's ultimate plan is success in the final wedding of the New Jerusalem, which is to be held between Jesus and His believers upon His return.

The first wedding in human history that the Bible records is that of Adam and Eve.

> "So the LORD God caused the man to fall into a deep sleep; and while he was sleeping, he took one of the man's ribs and then closed up the place with flesh. Then the LORD God made a woman from the rib he had taken out of the man, and he brought her to the man."

(Genesis 2:21-23)

Apostle Paul interprets the marriage of Adam and Eve as the following.

"[⋯] as Adam, who is the pattern of the one to come."
(Romans 5:14)

"For this reason a man will leave his father and mother and be united to his wife, and the two will become one flesh. This is a profound mystery – but I am talking about Christ and the church."
(Ephesians 5:31-32)

As the influential Welsh Protestant minister Martyn Lloyd-Jones once said, the wedding of Adam and Eve foreshadows the final wedding banquet of Revelations 21 between Jesus and the church. In other words, Adam represents Jesus and Eve represents the church.

Just as Jesus died on the cross to gain the church as His bride, so does Adam die to gain Eve as his wife. The marriage of Adam and Eve begins with the death of Adam. In Genesis 2, God, after creating Adam, puts him into a deep sleep. The Hebrew origin of the word "to sleep" is "to die." Only after Adam's death did God take one of his ribs to create Eve. When Jesus was hung on the cross of Calvary, a soldier pierced his ribs with a spear, and blood and water gushed out. Just as Adam earned Eve by giving up his rib, so did Jesus earn us, as His bride, by giving up his blood and water.

> "Instead, one of the soldiers pierced Jesus' side with a spear, bringing a sudden flow of blood and water."
> (John 19:34)

The true image of a married couple is the image of Jesus and the church. Just because a man and woman live together for a lifetime does not make them united.

As the death of Adam created Eve and the death of Jesus birthed the church, similarly, husbands, in gaining their wives, must *die*. Only when the husband dies can he earn the heart of his wife. Every husband must learn to die for his wife. This is a death to *self*, a death to selfish desires, and a death to pride. Husbands, are you willing to die for the wife you love?

> "Husbands, love our wives, just as Christ loved the church and gave himself up for her."
> (Ephesians 5:25)

The death of the husband calls for an equally appropriate response from the wife. Apostle Paul calls this appropriate response *obedience*.

> "Submit to one another out of reverence for Christ. Wives, submit yourselves to your own husbands as you do to the Lord. For the husband is the head of the wife as Christ is the head of the church, his body, of which he is the Savior. Now as the church submits to Christ, so also wives should submit to their husbands in everything."
> (Ephesians 5:22–24)

Wives, do you truly desire for this man to become your husband? Then, you must learn to obey. There is no happiness without obedience. We must learn obedience toward our husbands at home and our pastors at church. We need to remember that the highest virtue of a woman is obedience, and this virtue not only ends in the marriage of the flesh but also extends to the final wedding banquet of the Lamb.

Through the joys and sorrows experienced in physical marriage, we must remember the final wedding with Jesus. Through the joys and sorrows of marriage, we must hold onto Jesus and grow to be more like Him. This is what a wise bride preparing for the eternal Kingdom of God looks like!

Chapter 10
Where Is My Isaac?

Where are my Adam, my Isaac, and my Enoch? Where is my future spouse?

Even in the first marriage of mankind, it was not Adam and Eve but God, the Governor of all encounters, who initiated the relationship.

> "Then the LORD God made a woman from the rib he had taken out of the man, and he brought her to the man."
> (Genesis 2:22)

Marriage is not arranged by our own strength. It is planned, led, and accomplished by the guidance of God. We must trust in God alone who makes possible our success in both the marriage of the physical and of the New Jerusalem. This is the biblical principle of marriage.

In Genesis 24, the Bible captures the marriage story of a wise woman who was aware of this principle. This woman's name was Rebekah.

Rebekah

Genesis 24 delivers a powerful message about how the Triune God is actively involved in our journey toward marriage. Genesis 24 describes the journey of Abraham in his search, through his servant Eliezer, for a daughter-in-law who would be wed to his one and only son, Isaac.

To Abraham, the marriage of Isaac was of great significance. Marriage was not a mere passing down of physical lineage but an important passing down of the covenant that God had made with Abraham to make him into a great nation for the redemptive work of Jesus. Knowing this, Abraham commands his servant Eliezer to find a daughter-in-law not in the idol-filled Canaanite land but in Abraham's hometown, Paddan Aram. Abraham, in leading the redemptive plan of the Messiah through the marriage of Isaac and Rebekah, represents *Father God*.

> "'I want you to swear by the LORD, the God of heaven and the God of earth, that you will not get a wife for my son from the daughters of the Canaanites, among whom I am living, but will go to my country and my own relatives and get a wife for my son Isaac.'"
>
> (Genesis 24:3–4)

After receiving Abraham's command, Eliezer (whose name means "Helper" or "Help of my God") prays and acts to fulfill the will of his master. During the days of his journey, Eliezer continues to pray to God for signs indicating the woman of God's will. Before Eliezer even finishes praying, God answers his prayers by leading Rebekah to him. Eliezer, who actively searches for and guides Rebekah to Isaac, as Abraham commanded, represents our helper, the *Holy Spirit*.

> "Then he prayed, 'LORD, God of my master Abraham, make me successful today, and show kindness to my master Abraham.'"
> (Genesis 24:12)

Isaac, who is meditating in the fields while waiting for his bride to arrive, is Abraham's one and only son. Having obeyed his father on Mount Moriah in Genesis 22, Isaac is a son of obedience who, through his obedience to death, becomes the rightful heir to the covenant of God with Abraham. Isaac represents God's one and only son, *Jesus*, who died on the cross and became the rightful heir to all authority in heaven and on earth. Just as Isaac was comforted by his marriage to Rebekah, so Jesus finds the greatest joy in his marriage to us.

> "Isaac brought her into the tent of his mother Sarah, and he married Rebekah. So she became his wife, and he loved her; and Isaac was comforted after his mother's death."
> (Genesis 24:67)

Finally, the beautiful bride, Rebekah, is revealed. Rebekah was the woman whom God had chosen to become Isaac's wife. But at the time of Eliezer's calling, Rebekah knew nothing about Isaac's appearance and height or character and temperament. But the moment she confirms that this marriage is God's will, Rebekah surrenders her thoughts, emotions, and will to immediately follow Eliezer. With a beauty surpassing that of any other woman, Rebekah was fully capable of finding pleasure and luxuriating in the lusts of the world. But just as Adam earned Eve through his death, Rebekah earns, through her obedience to God's will, Isaac and a destiny of fulfilling the covenant of God. Rebekah is the beautiful image of us, *Christ's believers*, as brides to our bridegroom, Jesus.

> "So they called Rebekah and asked her, 'Will you go with this man?' 'I will go,' she said."
> (Genesis 24:58)

According to Pastor Jun, the journey to marriage is not passively waiting for Prince Charming. Rather, the journey to marriage is actively preparing to discover and obey God's will. It is a time of preparing our hearts to recognize that the will of God always gives us hope and a future.

> "'For I know the plans I have for you,' declares the LORD, 'plans to prosper you and not to harm you, plans to give you hope and a future.'"
> (Jeremiah 29:11)

But why is it so difficult for us to believe in the goodness of God's will? This is because it is not God but the *self* that remains the owner of our thoughts, emotions, values, philosophies, and sense of will. Ever since the original sin of Adam and Eve, the very essence of the *self*, or human nature, has changed. In the fallen, selfish, and self-centered man, there exists no perfect standard, no perfect judgment, and no perfect rationale. That is why to follow the perfect will of God, we need to acknowledge our fallenness and reset our standards to God's Word.

Like Rebekah, who responded immediately to the calling of Eliezer, we must be sensitive to the voice, emotions, and conscience that the Holy Spirit creates inside of us. In a constant relationship with God, such spiritual sensitivity to the Holy Spirit begins to grow.

A daily commitment to worship, read the Bible, and pray is the foundation of a relationship with God. Many Christians habitually attend church and religiously practice prayer. But a life of true Christianity grows through time spent with God, getting to know Him more deeply today than I did yesterday and more deeply tomorrow than I did today. Only those who personally experience God can trust His perfect will, which, at times, can be difficult to understand.

How is your relationship with God, right now? There is a good question that can provide the most accurate assessment of your current relationship with God.

"Who is God to you?"

Chapter 11
Who is God to You?

Who is God to you? Is He one who unconditionally loves and acknowledges you? Or is He fearsome and authoritative? Is He one who listens to even your smallest groans? Or is He busy and absent? Is He one who will be with you forever? Or will He one day forsake you?

Ever since sin entered the world through the disobedience of Adam and Eve, all mankind is born with a distorted view of who God is. Due to the broken environment we grow up in, the family and people around us, and the various events and accidents we experience, we develop a faulty portrait of God, radically impacting our relationship with Him. In particular, our relationship with our *physical father* most affects our relationship with our *spiritual Father*, God. For example, children raised by an authoritative father end up viewing

God as an authority figure rather than the gentle and loving Father that He is. Children raised by a weak and timid father end up viewing God as incompetent, insecure, and unreliable.

Today, many parents do not acknowledge their responsibility for the wounds of their children. This neglect of unresolved scars leads adolescents to develop distorted perceptions of God and, consequently, to distance themselves from God. This is an unfortunate reality of church youth today.

Although this reality was what I, too, had experienced in my relationship with God, what significantly transformed my lukewarm and religious life into an intimate and personal relationship was a powerful encounter I had with God. What was this encounter? And where did it all start?

What started this transformation was a question that my mother asked me when I was in the seventh grade of middle school.

"Mary, who is God to you?"

Such a question, I had never heard in my life. I pondered hard and, after a minute or so, answered.

"Well, God is a good father, but at the same time, He's a strict one. It's like He only gives me vegetables that are good for the body but never gives me what I actually want."

Surprised by my answer, my mother remained silent for

a while, after which she asked me again.

"Mary, why do you think that God is strict and doesn't give you what you want? The God that I know isn't like that at all. Let's ask the Holy Spirit. The Holy Spirit will surely tell you why when you ask in prayer."

> "But the Advocate, the Holy Spirit, whom the Father will send in my name, will teach you all things and will remind you of everything I have said to you."
> (John 14:26)

Praying in tongues, I asked the Holy Spirit. And in a minute or so, old memories, which I could not possibly have made up on the spot, began to unfold before my closed eyes just like a movie reel. The first memory that the Holy Spirit revealed to me was of when I was in the first grade of elementary school in Michigan. At a familiar supermarket in a familiar aisle, I was holding a toy, asking my mother if I could buy it. Then, in a memory as vivid as if it had happened only days before, my mother answered me.

"Mary, is this a need or want? Is this something you

really need, or is it just something you want?"

This is a question that I, while growing up, most frequently heard from my mother. Living abroad in America as a poor Korean immigrant family, my mother, even while working two jobs, had to strictly save to support both my father's seminary schooling and maintain our standard of living. At a young age, I had understood the circumstances of our family and so, had always returned the toys that I had wanted so badly. But the strict teachings of my mother during my childhood had subconsciously influenced how I viewed my spiritual parent, God. To me, God, though protective and wise, was a strict and distant being.

As I shared the memories that the Holy Spirit had revealed to me, I began shedding tears. Though my mother was the person whom I loved most in the world, I realized that there were scars in my heart toward her that I had never recognized before. From her telling me to "hurry, hurry," refusing to buy me what I wanted as a child, and requiring a fast-paced and obedient upbringing, I had been *hurt*. As the shedding of tears turned into heavy weeping, I opened my mouth to confess to her my honest feelings.

"Mom, it really wasn't easy for me."

Vomiting out all my emotions and saying everything that I had suppressed as a young child, I felt free and refreshed. It was then that my mother said something that was to change my life forever.

"Mary, I'm so sorry."

That day, my relationship with my mother was restored. And that day, my relationship with God, too, was restored, as I realized that God was not the same as my physical parents. Though my physical parents were imperfect, God is a perfect Father. God is neither busy, nor poor, nor strict. He listens to my smallest groans, heeds every emotion, and provides for me in times of need.

Our greatest priority is seeing God for who He really is. A personal encounter with God inspires dreams, unlocks unimaginable abilities, and gives freedom and joy. And above all else, a personal relationship with God builds in us a strength to trust in the will of God regardless of what it may seem or sound like. *If God loves me so, how would He misguide me?*

During my struggles to trust God's will in my marriage to Enoch, God spoke to me about His relationship with me.

"Mary, focus on me! Who am I to you?"

"You …?"

"If you, then, though you are evil, know how to give good gifts to your children, how much more will your Father in heaven give good gifts to those who ask him!"
(Matthew 7:11)

What makes possible our obedience to God's will is the personal trust that is built in our continual relationship with Him. It was this relationship with God that gave me unconditional trust that Enoch, of whom I knew neither appearance nor personality, was the best companion that God had planned for me.

Chapter 11 Who is God to You?

Chapter 12
I Feel Comfortable When I'm Around You

"One day, you're going to end up liking me!"

In terms of personality, I had never been the one to initiate or first express any romantic feeling or relationship. But as soon as I realized that marriage to Enoch was God's will, God began to change my words and actions. Whenever I met Enoch, the Holy Spirit would prompt me in the words to say, and I was more than delighted to obey.

"Enoch, you have great talent."

"Enoch, God has a beautiful plan for you."

"Enoch, you know that I like you, but do you know how much more God loves you?"

All these words were things that I would only have said

to someone I was dating!

On any day that I was to go out on a date with Enoch, I prepared myself in prayer before leaving the house.

"God, what should I ask Enoch today? I want to get to know him more."

During the one month that I went on dates with Enoch, I asked him *everything*. From his Myers-Briggs Type Indicator (MBTI) personality type, blood type, favorite and least favorite foods, favorite sport, taste in music, love languages, experiences studying abroad in America, relationship with his parents and siblings, memories of his grandparents, saddest memory, and dreams and vision for the future all the way to his current relationship with God. While listening to him talk, I would pay attention not only to the words he spoke but also to his eyes, body language, and even the tone of his voice to recognize when he was most happy, sad, excited, or discouraged. Such conversational wisdom was possible not because I had majored in psychology but because God had given me wisdom when I sought him in prayer. God gave me not only wisdom but also the courage and confidence in getting to know Enoch. With every step I took, I felt that God was pleased with my faith. From the moment we know the will of God in marriage, we need to start actively moving in faith.

Among the many, the greatest step of faith I took was when I held Enoch's face and confessed my feelings to him in the car.

"One day, you're going to end up liking me!"

That night, on which I had cried out to God in the greatest sorrow while driving home, was the same night that Enoch began to have feelings for me.

Just like me, Enoch had been in a dating relationship

for a long time. But at the words of His parents that the relationship was not God's will, he, too, had chosen to obey and break up. That is why on the first day we met, we were able to relate to one another as we shared our testimonies. In the end, such honest conversations and strong similarities in our faith journeys ended up creating mutual feelings of admiration and affection for one another. Though I did not know then, the Holy Spirit had already begun to open Enoch's heart from the first day we met, weeks before my confession in the car.

In just two weeks, Enoch, who personality-wise would only express his feelings after building a friendship over an extended period of time, began to express his affection toward me. And in just one month, just like Pastor Jun had prayed, Enoch proposed to me a lifelong journey as a married couple. For Enoch, liking someone in two weeks and loving someone enough to commit to a marriage in just a single month was absolutely unthinkable. But according to Enoch, with every moment he spent with me, he saw himself change in ways that he had never thought were possible in the past. As someone who could never show his most honest self to anyone, even his ex-girlfriend, Enoch was surprised to find that within just a week of dating me, he was completely able to be his real self. And as someone who had once thought wearing glasses was unattractive, Enoch was surprised to find himself starting to think that I, in my everyday casualwear of jeans and a plaid shirt with bulky black glasses, looked pretty.

"Mary, I feel comfortable when I'm around you."

And so it was in this way that at the age of 24, I met the lifelong companion that God had planned for me all along. And just like Pastor Jun had prayed, Enoch and I, after one month of dating, got married on October 5th, 2021.

But after marriage, I had one final question for God.

"God, You could have led us to one another in a more natural way, like how most people meet. But, why did you not?"

"Mary."

"Yes?"

"Don't you know that you have gained so much more?"

"Gained so much more?" When I gave my everything, along with my marriage decision, to God by faith, God had given His everything to me. By giving my independent thoughts, emotions, and will to God, I not only met Jesus as my eternal bridegroom but also, as I would realize as I began my married life, received the husband of my prayers.

Enoch, whom I had chosen in faith, had, in him, the answers to the prayers I had prayed to God as a young girl.

Chapter 13
Mary's <Future Husband> Prayer List

Ever since the sixth grade of middle school, I had prayed for my future husband. As the years passed, up until I reached the age of 24, I found myself praying for a list of 30 items. The following is my prayer list.

All encounters begin in the hands of God. Therefore, it is God whom we must seek for His blessing in relationships. There is not a single prayer to God that ever falls on deaf ears. Even though we cannot yet see God's answer to our prayers, God will answer every prayer that He hears.

> "So tell them, 'As surely as I live, declares the LORD, I will do to you the very thing I heard you say.'"
> **(Numbers 14:28)**

Though all I did was pray for my future spouse for ten

1. One who loves God more than his life and loves me, our children, parents, neighbors, and country with the love of God.
2. One who has passion for the Kingdom of God and a passion for me.
3. One who is humble and holy, with a spirit of martyrdom.
4. One who has a gifting of prayer and preaching God's Word.
5. One who is professionally equipped and respected in society.
6. One who is gentle and healed of all inner scars.
7. One who has a bigger heart than mine to have patience with me.
8. One who is filled with the Holy Spirit and is able to spiritually discern.
9. One who takes care of his body for God's work.
10. One who is easygoing.
11. One whose parents can be coworkers in God's work.
12. One whose mother enjoys cooking.
13. One who speaks positively.
14. One who is gifted in financial management.
15. One who always hugs me and holds my hand.
16. One who loves worshiping daily.
17. One who praises God in any circumstance.
18. One who does not have double eyelids.
19. One who is humble enough to cover my parents' flaws.
20. One who wants to share my vision.
21. One who admires nature.
22. One who always tells me that I am beautiful.
23. One who is patient enough to listen to my talkative sister.
24. One who seeks the voice of God every morning.
25. One who asks God, even in the smallest decisions.
26. One who is bold like a lion in public and sweet like a lamb at home.
27. One who attends the early morning service every day.
28. One who has big dreams yet puts family first.
29. One who treats sons and daughters with the same love.
30. One who is like pure gold.

years, God blessed me in three powerful ways. First, it was I who began changing in accordance with my prayers. While praying for my future husband, I found God shaping me to be like pure gold. Second, God answered me with the man of my prayers. In all the small and big requests to God, God answered. Third, God made me realize that marriage is not about immediate perfection but, instead, about a *progress* toward *gradual* perfection. As of right now, neither Enoch nor I is a perfect manifestation of our prayers. However, we must learn to see each other not with disappointment in present flaws but with hope for future growth. This is how God sees us.

We call this type of perception *future reality*. This means a perception in which one looks at the other with faith in God's promise and treats the other with words of encouragement and acknowledgment, as if the future change is already the present reality. Regardless of every weakness we see in our spouse, God has a strong and powerful promise for that life. It is this heart of future reality that God wants us to share in our married life. With this heart, we must be coworkers in God's plan for our spouse by continuing to encourage and lift them up. It is true that every spouse has his or her downsides. However, when God's will is what is emphasized and encouraged, the good attributes grow, and the negative ones fade away. It is God who works in our spouse to fulfill His good purpose, and it is our job to live by faith.

> "For it is God who works in you to will and to act in order to fulfill his good purpose."
>
> (Philippians 2:13)

From the first day that I met Enoch until now, I pray for him every day, and to a wife of prayer, God chose to reveal His heart. Below is a summary not of my opinionated judgment but of God's revelation of who Enoch is.

First, Enoch is a gentle but strong man. Growing up, Enoch was a child of much loneliness. With a minister father and a piano accompanist mother, Enoch's parents were absent six days a week, preaching and doing revival work in churches all across South Korea. In the absence of his parents, it was Enoch's grandmother who raised him with unconditional and sacrificial love. Until age 11, Enoch grew up under his grandmother, after which God sent him to study abroad at his aunt's house in California. Completely different from his grandmother, Enoch's aunt strictly taught him discipline and self-management. A few years later, Enoch enrolled in a military boarding school, at which he came across the sport of American football, which would completely change his shy and timid personality. In a God-led encounter with the high school's football coach, Enoch was forced to join the football team. Though at times he was ignored as the only Asian on the team, Enoch did not give up and eventually graduated as team captain. As this shows, Enoch has a gentle but strong heart of tenacity and perseverance.

Second, Enoch is a family man. As a psychology major,

I realize that the most accurate personality type test is the MBTI. Of the 16 MBTI personality types, I am an ENFJ and Enoch is an ISFJ. On the second date that I went on with Enoch, we took the MBTI test on his phone, and, looking at the results, Enoch laughed in utter amazement at how accurate they were. I was no less surprised, as the MBTI type that Enoch matched was the personality type I had prayed for.

According to the results, Enoch is an ISFJ (introverted, sensing, feeling, and judging), the *Protector* personality type. The Protector is a kind of person that most closely resembles the ideal parent. Caring for others in kindness, dedication, and unswerving commitment is the Protector's greatest desire.

For the Protector, starting and building a family is life's greatest priority, sometimes more important than personal career achievement. Of the 30 items on my prayer list, this is the 28th that God answered. Among all 16 personality types, the Protector is the most ideal parent type and the most ideal spouse. Even today, though I never ask him, Enoch takes care of the majority of the housework: running the vacuum cleaner, cleaning the toilet, sorting the garbage, and folding the laundry. Enoch, while casually humming, joyfully dedicates himself to the family. To someone like me, who often puts God's work ahead of the family, Enoch is God's providence and grace.

What surprised me most when I met Enoch was that he had all the positive attributes of both my ex-boyfriend and the one whom I had liked before meeting Enoch. With a college degree in applied mathematics, my ex-boyfriend was a very rational, mathematical, and fact-based person. Though his rational personality did fill the gaps in my more intuitive inclinations, many times did I find myself exhausted because of his heavy rationalism. But Enoch, though sharing the same rational thinking, is more emotional. This supports a healthy balance in our relationship.

The person I liked before meeting Enoch was a very emotional person, writing me strings of letters and personal notes of encouragement. Unlike my ex-boyfriend, who was less expressive, this person was accustomed to expressing his feelings through words, both spoken and written. But Enoch, whom most people would assume, based on his physical appearance, to be cold and inexpressive, not only writes me letters but also texts me multiple times throughout the day just to express his love and affection. Even more, Enoch loves to spend time together talking. With almost 70 percent of our conversation being Enoch's portion, I often find myself smiling at the talkative Enoch and pondering, "I wonder how much happier God is to see Enoch." To both God and me, Enoch is the apple of our eye.

Many times, I find Enoch filling in the gaps in my personality. Not sharing a keen interest in shopping for clothes, I find Enoch going out of his way to take me shopping. Not particularly skilled in accounting and office-based work or handling machines and electronic devices, I find Enoch teaching me with expertise. Enoch is the answer to my prayers and a real testimony to the living God.

Third, whatever he does, Enoch does as to the Lord. Even while studying abroad in America, Enoch worked part-time jobs every summer when he would return home to Korea. Although he was not in immediate need of money, Enoch did not want to waste the time that he was given. For the eight years of studying abroad, Enoch worked part-time jobs, ranging from being a parking lot cart attendant, fast-food worker, convenience store clerk, and textile factory worker to being a teriyaki restaurant worker. But what is more surprising is that in each industry, he was promoted from a low-level employee to an assistant manager in just a month or two. When he had to return to America at the end of his summer breaks, the bosses in all his workplaces offered him a higher weekly wage in order to keep him.

It turns out that whatever Enoch did, he did as to the Lord. Working as a parking lot cart attendant, Enoch would pull 17 carts at one time when the typical worker pulled ten. Working as a fast-food employee, Enoch would go beyond his designated role as a cashier clerk to help move heavy boxes when others were reluctant. Working as a convenience store clerk, Enoch would restock products as soon as they were sold when others would typically wait until the end of their shift. Working as a textile factory worker, Enoch would complete a day's worth of packaging and go beyond to help the boss with their personal work, to the point where the boss had full confidence in Enoch to even entrust him with the factory keys. Compared to those workers who only did what is required of them, Enoch caught the attention of the many bosses he worked for because of his attitude. During his time working at a teriyaki restaurant, the owner had even entrusted Enoch with the store's accounting book and password. Unlike people who work to the minimum requirement, Enoch works as if he does it for the Lord. And God, seeing the sincerity and honesty of Enoch's heart of service, has given to him gifts of outstanding leadership and management—just like Joseph in the Old Testament.

Every time I pray for my husband, there is a person in the Bible that God reminds me of—Joseph. As the 11th son of Jacob, Joseph was Jacob's most beloved son, wearing long, colored robes worn only by managers. But at the age of 17, Joseph was sold into slavery in Egypt by his jealous brothers and became a servant in the house of Potiphar, the chief of Pharaoh's bodyguards. As a son of a wealthy family sold into slavery by his brothers, Joseph must have felt hopeless. Brought as a slave to a land with a foreign language, culture, and people, Joseph must have wanted to give up in the face of a hopeless reality. He could have lamented his circumstances and forever remained resentful of God.

But Joseph, even in the face of hardship, did not give up. He neither complained nor resented God. God was with Joseph, not only when he was the beloved son of a wealthy family but also when he was an impoverished and oppressed slave in Egypt. And because God was with Joseph, Joseph began to prosper in everything he did. This soon caught even the eyes of a worldly man like Potiphar who did not believe in God. Seeing that God's hand was on Joseph, Potiphar promoted Joseph as the overseer of all his possessions.

> "Joseph found favor in his eyes and became his attendant. Potiphar put him in charge of his household, and he entrusted to his care everything he owned."
> (Genesis 39:4)

For those who are faithful in the small things, God entrusts the greater. In order to fulfill His plan of entrusting Joseph with not a single household but the entire nation of Egypt, God allowed the false accusation of the wife of Potiphar. Though having loyally worked for Potiphar for 11 years, Joseph, at age 28, was abandoned by his master and became a prisoner. Though demoted from the status of a slave to that of a prisoner, Joseph's life was still perfectly and intricately in God's control.

The prison to which Joseph was sent was for Egyptian politicians only. In this prison, God began to teach Joseph the politics and laws of Egypt. Under God's guidance, which at many times is incomprehensible to the human mind, Joseph remained faithful to the circumstances allowed by God. And because of the God who was with him, Joseph was once again entrusted with everything under the prison warden's care.

> "The warden paid no attention to anything under Joseph's care, because the LORD was with Joseph and gave him success in whatever he did."
> (Genesis 39:23)

In the place where others saw no hope, God arranged for Joseph a meeting that would forever change his life. In this place, Joseph met and interpreted the dreams of the cupbearer and baker. Two years later, at the cupbearer's mention, Joseph came before Pharaoh and interpreted his dreams, resulting in him becoming the prime minister of the great empire, Egypt, at the mere age of 30.

> "Joseph was thirty years old when he entered the service of Pharaoh king of Egypt. And Joseph went out from Pharaoh's presence and traveled throughout Egypt."
> (Genesis 41:46)

Because of the God who was with him, Joseph went from being a slave and overseer of an Egyptian household to a prisoner and, ultimately, a prime minister of the Egyptian empire. The 13 years of faithfulness to the incomprehensible guidance of God was not time wasted. This time, though seemingly long and utterly turbulent, was what was required to build the faith, character, and ability of Joseph to manage an entire nation's livelihood. This perfect plan had chosen the young, 13-year-old Joseph to be sold into Egypt in order to fulfill the covenant that God made with Abraham—the covenant of Jesus Christ. Through Joseph, who shares in the glory of God by becoming prime minister of Egypt, the 12 sons of Israel are gathered to this fruitful land in which they become a great nation for 400 years.

> "Call to me and I will answer you and tell you great and unsearchable things you do not know."
>
> (Jeremiah 33:3)

Chapter 14
Two Qualities of a Beautiful Bride

Ever since I was young, I wanted to get married early. So, upon enrolling in college, I began to make efforts in areas that I had previously not paid much attention to. To make my naturally round face into one that was slimmer, I attempted my first diet. To appear more feminine, I packed away my t-shirts and sweatpants and wore, for the first time, skirts and flowery dresses. And to appear more physically attractive, I went beyond the most basic lotion and sunscreen routine to start applying real makeup.

But two years after graduating from college, I found myself having gained weight, only wearing dull black suits every day, and experiencing adult acne due to a busy work-study schedule. And in such circumstances was when I met Enoch for the first time.

If physical appearance was really what was most important in marriage, I would have been disqualified at the first cut-off. The reason that I, despite the seeming flaws of my outward appearance, was able to approach Enoch with confidence and win his heart was that I had prepared two important qualities in myself. Though invisible to the physical eye, the two qualities that can surpass even physical appearance are a *relationship with God* and a *dream-oriented life*.

• The First Quality: A Relationship With God

The ministers, teachers, and workers at Sarang Jeil Church challenge and inspire me. Among the many, I find myself most inspired by Youth Pastor Lee Young-han because he, too, obeyed God's will in marrying his wife. Surrendering our thoughts and emotions to the often incomprehensible will of God is not an easy thing to do. For a person to give up his or her entire life to God is not easy. It is not by a sudden resolution or emotional fling that one obeys God's will but by the fruit of a lasting relationship with God that one can live out such faith. Such a man is Pastor Lee Young-han.

The following words are what Pastor Lee once preached to his young adults during an evening Bible study.

"To meet a good person, I, first, must become a good person."

Many people desire to meet a good person. But many do not try to become a good person themselves. There is a common saying in Korea that as the flies gather in the sewers and the butterflies flock to the flowers, so do we meet people like ourselves. People with a sweet aroma are similarly attracted to those with the same fragrance, whereas those with a bad odor end up surrounded by those with the same malodor. Therefore, in order to meet a good person in any relationship, we need to first become a person with a sweet aroma ourselves.

Then, how do we become people with a *pleasing aroma*?

"But thanks be to God, who always leads us as captives in Christ's triumphal procession and uses us to spread the aroma of the knowledge of him everywhere. For we are to

God the pleasing aroma of Christ among those who are being saved and those who are perishing."

(2 Corinthians 2:14-15)

A person with a pleasing aroma is not someone with good looks or a high intelligence quotient. A person with a pleasing aroma is someone with *a relationship* with Jesus.

Having a relationship with Jesus refers to our *faith*. Many people think that the Christian faith is a measure of a series of religious activities, such as the number of services attended, amount of time prayed, and pages of the Bible read. Of course, all these are fruits of our relationship with Jesus. But the true purpose of our worshiping, praying, and reading of the Bible is, through

Jesus, to experience a *restored unity* with our Father God.

> "Jesus answered, 'I am the way and the truth and the life. No one comes to the Father except through me.'"
>
> (John 14:6)

The ultimate goal of the Christian faith is *to know Father God*. The more we know God, the more we are filled with His love and restored to His image that was lost in the Garden of Eden. God's love quenches all thirst. And only those who have experienced such a love do not seek the acceptance or thirst for the acknowledgment of people. Only those who have experienced such a love can be confident in any circumstance. The faces of these people shine, and the words of these people build up others. Of such people we say, they have a pleasing aroma, and of such lives we say, they are bringing heaven down to earth.

Another reason why we must first focus on building a relationship with God is because when we stand upright in faith, we begin to see people with a different set of standards that are based on those of God. In praying for a future spouse, there are important requirements that we need to keep in mind. As Pastor Jun always says, the first condition for choosing a spouse is *faith*. No matter how much money and how reputable an academic background, a marriage without spiritual connection gives rise to conflict in all areas of both the married and personal life. But even though lacking in everything, if a couple shares the same faith in Christ, there is nothing that they cannot overcome. Shared faith is the first foundation of a happy marriage. Once this primary requirement is met, the additional conditions to consider when choosing a spouse are *personality, shared goals, and relationships*. Does the person have interests and habits similar to mine? Is the person's life oriented in a direction similar to mine? What kind of people does the person hang out and spend time with? This wisdom in choosing a spouse is not given by the world but by God in our constant relationship with Him.

- ### The Second Quality: A Dream-Oriented Life

Having a dream has a big influence on our daily lives. By leading a dream-oriented life, we, like Joseph in the Old Testament, can overcome the temptations of sin, transcend hardships, and, above all, recognize the will of God.

The fact that I also had a dream was the decisive reason why I was able to recognize God's will for my marriage to Enoch. The reason why I decided to break up with my ex-boyfriend and get rid of the feelings I had for the new person who had appeared before me was because I realized that they were not the ones with whom I could achieve the dream that God had given me. And the reason why I decided to marry Enoch, whom I had never met, was because I realized that this person was the one with whom I could achieve the dream that God had given me. Such a realization was neither a moment's rationale nor a fling of emotion. Rather, it was a conviction from the 10 years that I had prayed for the dreams that God had given me. And what most profoundly gave me conviction was God's answer to my prayer for a specific type of parents-in-law.

Ever since I was a kid, I remember my mother saying that the quickest way to recognize the ins and outs of a person you encounter is to meet their parents. As children are the fruit of their parents, one's parents tell us a lot about that individual.

Ever since I was young, I did not want to marry into an ordinary family but a family with parents-in-law who could support my ministry. That was why, as a kid, I had always wanted to marry the son of a Levite family—a pastor's kid. But as time passed, I began to give up such hopes because I thought that such a marriage would limit me in my vision of becoming a Christian businesswoman and politician. But in meeting Pastor Jun for the first time in August of 2020, I was shocked because in this pastor of a typical presbyterian church, there was everything that I had prayed for and dreamt of for the past ten years. In him, there was a vision of preaching God's Word to all nations, building business missions, and unifying South and North Korea. This conviction in Pastor Jun was what gave me the last answer that I needed in opening my heart to God's will: Enoch.

Had I not had this dream, I would have wasted more time in recognizing Enoch as God's will. In this way, having a dream is one of the most important qualities for recognizing a spouse. But other than recognizing our future spouse, there are several other reasons why we must have a dream.

Surprisingly, many people live their lives unaware of the necessity of having a dream. Even without dreams, people seem to get a good job, attract a decent spouse, and live a happy life. Then, why do we even need a dream?

First, having or not having a dream greatly affects our attitude toward the present. It is not an understatement that both our past and future are determined by our attitude toward the present. A person without a dream worries about the future and dwells on the past. On the other hand, a person with a dream achieves the goals of the future and corrects wrong decisions of the past. What determines this attitude is having or not having a dream.

Second, living a life without a dream is not the original image of man that God created. When God created mankind, He created them in His image and likeness. This image and likeness refer not necessarily to the physicality of God but to His character and traits.

> "Then God said, 'Let us make mankind in our image, in our likeness, so that they may rule over the fish in the sea and the birds in the sky, over the livestock and all the wild animals, and over all the creatures that move along the ground.'"
>
> (Genesis 1:26)

Who is God? God is not only Creator God, Almighty God, and Comforter God but He is also *Visionary God*. God's vision is the salvation of mankind, and He works relentlessly toward this redemptive plan. Therefore, it is innate in mankind, as the children of God, to dream dreams and envision visions.

As young kids growing up, we all had dreams. My dream in elementary school was to become a teacher, and Enoch's was to become a waste truck driver. As a young kid, I admired how teachers would share with us so much knowledge on the classroom whiteboards, and Enoch admired the man who drove the biggest car in town. Growing up, each kid has his or her own unique personality, interests, and dreams. But at some point, we begin to lose sight of even the smallest dream. What could the reason possibly be?

The reason why a kid of dreams becomes an adult of lost direction is because someone, at some time during that child's growth, clipped the child's wings that allowed them to dream, explore, and envision. The sharp remarks of people and the false values of the world begin to make one think that there is no hope in oneself and gradually make one give up on dreaming completely.

For a child of dreams to grow into an adult of direction and passion, the role of parents is very important. In other words, the people who make our dreams come true are our parents. When parents tolerate their children's mistakes, acknowledge their talents, and encourage growth, children are able to develop resilience and overcome new challenges.

Resilience refers to the strength of the mind in being able to recognize failure as a stepping stone to growth. In fact, according to a child psychology study, children who receive unconditional encouragement from their parents when growing up show less hesitation in solving difficult test questions compared to those who do not receive such parental encouragement. Children who receive more criticism than encouragement show a hesitation in solving problems, sometimes even completely avoiding a question if it is too difficult. Though equally capable, depending on the vocabulary and behavior of their parents, children can become either Nobel Prize winners or directionless wanderers. As parents, we need to encourage our children as they explore various interests and continue to believe in them even as they face challenges.

Though our parents encourage and nurture our dreams, they are not the ones who *give* dreams. If that is true, how on earth do we find our dreams? From whom do our dreams come?

Everything in this world has a purpose in creation. From the cutlery container to the drying rack, everything is created according to the inventor's intention. So are people. When God created us and planted us in our mother's womb, He had an intention. This intention, or purpose, we call God's *calling*.

Dreams are born when we meet the One who created us. When we hear from God the plans and thoughts He has for us, we begin to dream dreams and see visions. But many people regard God-given dreams as burdensome. They think that God-given dreams will weigh them down and force them to do difficult things. But we need to remember that God is our *Father*. Though it may be incomprehensible in the moment, just as parents give their children the best, God, too, gives us His best. Until the day we look back to realize the providence of God all along, we can be afraid of what is to come. But coming to God, trusting who He is, is what we call *faith*.

> "And without faith it is impossible to please God, because anyone who comes to him must believe that he exists and that he rewards those who earnestly seek him."
> (Hebrews 11:6)

In the sixth grade of middle school, I began to dream of becoming a global businesswoman and CEO to financially support pastors and missionaries. But at that time, I did not solemnly pray or desperately cling to God for a dream. Instead, what inspired me in this dream was my personal encounter with God. When I was in the sixth grade, my mother sent me on a week-long summer

Bible camp. It was during that week I experienced the love of Jesus on the cross for the first time and received the gift of tongues to pray. This powerful encounter with God's love toward a sinner like me not only made me cry for hours and hours but also ignited a purpose for my life. From the moment I realized God's love, I wanted to live for the One who loved me most.

In this way, in finding a dream, there is an *order*. Just as a church does not hand a mop to a new believer to clean the building floors, dreams should not be forced upon someone who has not yet personally met God, even if that someone may be your very own child.

Without love for God, we can neither grasp nor achieve the dreams that God gives us. For a child with no experience of God's love, the plans and purposes of God being preached to the child only create a burden. But when a child experiences the love of God, they begin to change. They begin to want to do something for God and start to trust God's plan for their life. Even if both these children receive the same dream, for the one who does not know God's love, the dream becomes a burden, and for the one who knows God's love, the dream becomes life's greatest blessing. Only those who have experienced God's love can realize the great blessing of God-given dreams and put their trust in His will.

"But those who hope in the LORD will renew their strength. They will soar on wings like eagles; they will run and not grow weary; they will walk and not be faint."
(Isaiah 40:31)

More than giving me a dream at a young age, God's love changed me to become motivated. Every day, I began to voluntarily read the Bible, worship, and pray in order to know more of who God was. Not only did I become motivated in my faith but I also became driven in my studies.

To be honest, I was not always the driven and motivated person that I am today. As a kid, I was neither smart nor talented compared to my classmates. But after a personal encounter with God in the sixth grade of middle school, I found a reason to study and work diligently. From then on, studying was no longer a burden but a joy! Though I could not afford, for financial reasons, afterschool hagwons and tutors like many of my friends could, I began to have faith that I could transcend all circumstances. With that faith, I gained a full scholarship for a private middle and high school in Seoul, which required about US$ 30,000 in tuition per year. And with that faith, I gained a full scholarship for a four-year private university, which required about US$ 70,000 in tuition per year. God's hand was over not only my academics but also my growth in musical and artistic talent. Serving whole-heartedly in the church, I experienced God giving me exponential growth of 100-, 60-, and 30-fold. Playing the piano and violin, conducting the choir, teaching Sunday school, and designing posters and videos, I saw exceptional musical talent and artistic taste in me that only God could have given.

Dreams and an attitude of positive motivation begin with God's love. That is why we need time to personally experience God. Without love for God, it is natural for everything to feel obligatory and burdensome. But just as we can do anything for the one whom we love most, the moment we realize the love of God, we end up not only studying and working for Him but also going beyond to give our entire life to Him.

"Who shall separate us from the love of Christ? Shall trouble or hardship or persecution or famine or nakedness or danger or sword?"

(Romans 8:35)

Then, how can we experience God's love?

Chapter 15
Parable of the Four Soils

Many Christians, even while attending church services and reading the Bible, do not feel the love of God. Why is this? Is it because God's love is conditional? Or because God's love is biased? Absolutely not! The answer to this question is found in the parable of the four soils in Matthew 13.

> "Then He told them many things in parables, saying: 'A farmer went out to sow his seed. As he was scattering the seed, some fell along the path, and the birds came and ate it up. Some fell on rocky places, where it did not have much soil. It sprang up quickly, because the soil was shallow. But when the sun came up, the plants were scorched, and they withered because they had no root. Other seed fell among thorns, which grew up and choked the plants. Still other seed fell on good soil, where it

produced a crop – a hundred, sixty or thirty times what was sown."

(Matthew 13:3-8)

In Matthew 13, Jesus talks about a farmer who goes out to sow his seed in four fields. The farmer is God, and the seed is God's Word. Though the farmer sows the exact same seeds, some soil is unable to even absorb the seed, whereas some soil not only absorbs the seed but also bears fruit up to a hundredfold what was sown. What do these fields symbolize, and why do they produce different outcomes?

The fields refer to our hearts. Everyone is different in how they absorb and experience God's Word. Though God loves everyone, the reason why we do not feel His love is because there is a problem *within us*—a problem in our field, or heart. Then, what kinds of hearts experience and do not experience God's love? Jesus describes this through the four types of fields.

The first type of field is the *path*. The path is a hardened type of soil because many people have trodden on it.

> "When anyone hears the message about the kingdom and does not understand it, the evil one comes and snatches away what was sown in their heart. This is the seed sown along the path."
>
> (Matthew 13:19)

The soil of the path is too hard and compact, and the sown seeds are unable to take root and are consequently snatched away and eaten by the birds. This state of heart is one that has been hardened and trampled by the words of people and so, though listening to God's Word, cannot absorb it. The Word of God lingers only for a short moment before the bird, which represents Satan, comes to devour it. People with a path-like heart commonly have an experience of growing up hearing the following words.

"You can't do it."

"You're helpless."

"You shouldn't have been born."

Though God calls us His beloved, people with a path-like heart have difficulty believing in God's love.

"God doesn't love me."

"God probably isn't interested in someone like me."

"God's love applies only to other people, not me."

The second type of field is the *rocky ground*. The rocky ground is filled with stones that block the roots from growing deep. Seeds sown in this thin soil quickly wither in the intense heat and die.

"The seed falling on rocky ground refers to someone who hears the word and at once receives it with joy. But since they have no root, they last only a short time. When trouble or persecution comes because of the word, they quickly fall away."

(Matthew 13:20–21)

The rocky ground shows that there are people who have rocks in their hearts. These rocks represent particular incidents in our lives that have caused lasting mental and emotional wounds. Such wounds can be from frequent fights between parents, divorce, domestic violence, bullying at school, sexual assault, family bankruptcy, and even the early death of a parent. These wounds gradually end up creating a distorted perception of who God is, and such faulty views of God ultimately prevent the absorption of God's Word. People with a rock-like heart initially receive God's Word with joy when coming to church but are soon discouraged by the difficulties of life.

"God isn't interested in me, just like my parents."

"God must be disappointed in me, like everyone else."

"God will someday forsake me too."

The third type of field is the soil of *thorns*. These thorns choke the sown seeds, stopping them from growing properly.

> "The seed falling among the thorns refers to someone who hears the word, but the worries of this life and the deceitfulness of wealth choke the word, making it unfruitful."
>
> (Matthew 13:22)

The field of thorns is a heart that does not bear fruit because it is already sown with the bad seeds of the world. Even before the seed of God's Word is sown, this field is covered with weeds and thorns. These thorns are the values of the world.

Let's think about this. There are 168 hours in one week. Assuming that we sleep seven hours a day, there are 140 active hours in a week. Those who only attend a Sunday service once a week hear the Word of God for a single hour and live the remaining 139 hours listening to the values of the world. Those who additionally attend a

Sunday evening service, Wednesday service, and Friday service end up spending 136 hours listening to the values of the world. Finally, those who, in addition, attend early morning prayer every weekday spend around 130 hours listening to the values of the world.

If we do not make a resolution in our faith to worship, read the Bible, and pray daily, the values of the world will end up dominating our faith. It is a mistake to assume that the moment we accept Jesus, the values of the world inside us instantly disappear. From the moment we accept Jesus, the Holy Spirit begins to work, through worship and prayer, to uproot the false values of the world. In the education of Israel, Israeli mothers teach their children, until they enroll in elementary school, *only* the Word of God. Israeli mothers teach them only the Word of God so that their children are able to filter the values that the world preaches. This is what wise parenting looks like.

The fourth type of field is the *good soil*. In this parable, Jesus describes the field that bears fruit as neither the path nor the rocky ground nor the thorny field but only the good soil.

> "But the seed falling on good soil refers to someone who hears the word and understands it. This is the one who produces a crop, yielding a hundred, sixty or thirty times what was sown."
> (Matthew 13:23)

Good soil is neither hard nor rocky nor thorny. It is fertile and fruitful, yielding a crop of a 100, 60, or 30 times what was sown. Thirty times, we need to remember, is absolutely not a small return.

It is not that there is something wrong with God when we cannot feel His love, but there is something wrong with *us* when we cannot feel His love. Nevertheless, God never forcibly opens our closed and wounded hearts. God tells us that this field, which represents our heart, belongs to us.

> "Here I am! I stand at the door and knock. If anyone hears my voice and opens the door, I will come in and eat with that person, and they with me."
> (Revelations 3:20)

God is almighty yet does not force us to open our closed hearts. God is strong yet does not recklessly till the fields of our hearts, ignoring whatever pain it causes. Then, how does God approach us? He *waits*. God waits for us to open our hearts by our own will. That is why it is we who must diligently cultivate the fields of our hearts to heal any unresolved wounds and broken relationships that are blocking us from opening our hearts to God. This is the key to bringing heaven down to earth.

"Truly I tell you, whatever you bind on earth will be bound in heaven, and whatever you loose on earth will be loosed in heaven."

(Matthew 18:18)

Then, how can we make our hearts to be of good soil?

To make good land, we must plow *everything*. That is by no means an easy thing to do. Sometimes, our most feared past, memory, or scar can be so painful to revisit. But this work must happen within us, and it is definitely not a one-time process.

Computers store the full picture of an event, but the human brain goes beyond this to store the corresponding emotion. This is an astonishing fact about the human brain. But what becomes a problem is that, over time, these stored emotions enter our subconscious thinking. That is why years later, in the face of events similar to those from the past, the brain triggers the contingent emotion. This becomes a problem when the emotion is negative, like frustration, depression, or anger. The type of situation in which negative emotions arise differs from person to person. Some people experience uncontrollable anger when they are compared to others, whereas other people experience the same emotion when they are ignored by others. These sudden eruptions often lead to unfortunate consequences, like losing a friend, going through a divorce, or shutting out a family member.

But sudden eruptions of unhealthy emotions are not without reason. In order to make good soil, the root causes must be discovered and removed. As in my case, the most common root cause of these negative emotions can be found in the childhood experiences we have with our parents.

Chapter 16
Mary, I'm Sorry

As a kid, I was always proud of my father. During my father's studies at Calvin Seminary in Michigan, my friends, who were also pastors' kids, were always envious of the sweet and fun father that I had. Ever since I can remember, my father has always been a man of unconditional love. Whenever I would make a mistake, he would pat me on the back to say that all was okay. Whenever I would trip and fall on the ground, he would rather kick the road lightly and scold it for having made me fall.

Looking back, I realize that the reason why I was able to view God as a loving and gracious Father was because my father, too, had been loving and gracious. Through my upbringing, my father had shown me a healthy image of what a father figure was, and this had allowed me to easily approach and personally meet God at a young age.

But in my freshman year of college, there was an incident that was to make me discover, for the first time, that there was a deep anger inside of me toward my father.

One day, several weeks into my first semester of college, my father called me on the phone. Excited to hear his voice in a land that I was now to live alone, I quickly picked up the phone.

"Hi, dad!"

I, excited to speak to him, was thrown off by what he said.

"Hi, Mary! Hold on a sec ···"

As soon as I heard the second half of his typical greeting, I knew what was to come next. My father, who is a pastor and evangelist, gives his life to sharing the Gospel. Spreading the Gospel is his greatest love and passion. So, even after we moved to Korea, whenever he would see English-speaking foreigners walking down the streets, he would always start a conversation and many times, make me, as a fluent English speaker, ask for the person's contact information. Even when at home, I would get random calls from my father only to talk to strangers. And these random calls always started with the following greeting.

"Hi, Mary! Hold on a sec ···"

But hearing such a greeting miles and miles away from home, I was infuriated like I had never been before. Though frustrated and annoyed, I put up with my emotions and continued the conversation on the phone. The phone call ended in less than a minute, but the anger inside of me would not subside. Even upon returning to Korea the next summer, I found myself erupting in anger at every request from my father.

Everything my father asked me to do bothered, frustrated, and angered me. Every request from him, asking me to design a poster for a church fundraising event, translate the weekly church announcement into English, or make videos to advertise for the upcoming revival meeting, utterly annoyed me. Ignoring, for the first time, his calls and text messages, I could not understand why I had changed so much. Back in middle and high school when he had asked me to do the same amount of work, I had never been angered. But why had I suddenly become a disrespectful daughter? I blamed everything on myself and, for weeks, tried to find the reason from inside of me. But that was not quite the answer.

One day, nearing the end of summer break, I walked up to my mother, who was praying on the pulpit after the Friday evening service. For the first time, I honestly explained to her the anger and frustration I was feeling. My mother neither scolded me nor ignored my feelings. After listening carefully, she instructed me in a way that was starkly different from that of other parents.

"Mary, let's ask the Holy Spirit."

"Huh?"

"The Holy Spirit reminds us and teaches us everything when we ask in prayer."

> "But the Advocate, the Holy Spirit, whom the Father will send in my name, will teach you all things and will remind you of everything I have said to you."
> (John 14:26)

Praying, I started asking the Holy Spirit in an audible voice.

"Holy Spirit, I feel frustrated and lost. Every time I see my dad, I get irritated, but I don't know what the problem is and how to even deal with these emotions. Holy Spirit, can you teach me why I have such negative feelings toward my dad? Please, tell me ⋯"

Not long after praying, the Holy Spirit showed me an image. It looked like an elementary school classroom that I had studied in while living in Michigan. In the image, I could see how, while all the other children were accompanied by both their father and mother, I was the only kid accompanied by one parent. Looking at my mother holding a camcorder in one hand and waving vigorously to me with the other, I was happy and thankful. But for the first time, looking at my childhood self, I realized the deep longing that I had always had from the absence of my father. Besides this, the Holy Spirit continued to show me a panoramic view of all the years of my childhood in America. At every ballet and violin recital, every weekend trip to the public library, and every dining table, it was always me and my mother.

Through prayer, the Holy Spirit revealed to me the reasons for my anger. Though my father was a man of love and acceptance, he, at the same time, had been a father who was absent throughout my life. With a big vision and passion for world missions, my father had planted a church even while studying at seminary school in America, then immediately planted another when our family moved to Korea in 2009. Leaving the house at 4:00 AM and returning at midnight, my father had always been busy, occupied, and absent. To me, the word *family* evoked an image of me, my mother, and our dog Eunshil—but no father.

Upon our return to Korea in 2009, my father immediately planted All Nations Disciple Church at which both my parents minister to this day, signaling the start of my *ministry* as a pastor's daughter. Attending church services, accompanying on the piano, performing on the violin, making PowerPoint slides for the praise team, folding Sunday service pamphlets, designing event posters, making advertising videos, and even washing the dishes, cleaning the floors, and disposing of food waste, the middle and high school years that I spent in Korea were times of obedience and training.

But strangely enough, when I was in middle and high

school, during which time adolescent puberty would normally hit hard, I could not get angry with my father. Seeing how small our church was and my father working day and night to make up for the lack of helping hands, I felt guilty for refusing any request related to church. To a father so loving and caring, I felt sorry for expressing any frustration or anger and, instead, suppressed my honest feelings. Over the years, these suppressed emotions and old scars began to create in me a deep anger and resentment toward my father.

During the summer break after my first year in college, the Holy Spirit helped me to realize that I had a deep and old resentment toward my father and that this unresolved resentment was what was causing the irritation and frustration in my daily interactions with him. That Friday when I spoke with my mother and received an answer from the Holy Spirit through prayer, my mother immediately suggested that I deal with this problem that very night. I decided to do so. When we got home, I sat on the living room floor waiting for my father to return. At midnight, like usual, my father came home. I told him that I had something to share with him and asked him to come to the living room. My father quickly changed his clothes and came out to the living room, sitting in front of me with surprised, round eyes.

"Dad, you're a really good father to me. You accept both my strengths and weaknesses, you compliment me all the time, and you encourage me in times of difficulty and hardship. But at some moment in time, I realized that there is a burning anger inside of me toward you. Every time you send me text messages of the next thing to translate into English, every time you hand the phone over to a complete stranger, and every time you ask me to do things for church, it annoys and angers me and even makes me ⋯ hate you."

"So today, after the evening service, I prayed to God about this. 'I love my dad so much, but why is there an unexplained anger inside of me?' As soon as I asked, the Holy Spirit revealed to me the reason why. Ever since I was little, you were always absent from my life. Even during my teenage years, you, instead of spending time with me, would always ask for work, work, and work every single day. Now, studying abroad in America, I naturally assume that every phone call that I get from you is another church-related request. And to be honest, there were probably more times when I ignored your calls and text messages than when I answered them."

I had never said anything like this to my father before. Even while saying such things, I felt sorry for my father and wondered if I was overreacting to something that was already of the past. But as soon as I finished talking, all the resentment and sadness that I had stored inside of me began to pour out in uncontrollable tears.

"Dad, do you know how hard it was for me to live as your daughter? All I wanted was, like all the other kids, to go on picnics and spend time together on the weekends …"

As I cried uncontrollably, my father, seeing his daughter cry for the first time, was shocked and opened his mouth to explain himself.

"Mary, you know how busy I was with my ministry. What I did for you was the best that I could. Don't you know how much I love you?"

At that moment, my mother, who had come over to

where we were sitting, stopped my father from talking.

"Just listen, listen."

In the silence, I cried and cried until all the sorrow inside of me was emptied. When all the emotions that I had suppressed over the many years were finally expressed that night, I felt a refreshment inside of me that I had never experienced before. It was as refreshing as having the air conditioner turned to the maximum. Wiping away my tears, I lifted my head to look at my father. Tears had welled up in his eyes, and he looked at me as he said his first words.

"Mary, I'm so sorry."

As soon as I heard his first words, I burst into a second round of tears. These tears were different from the first. These tears seemed to melt down the rock-like wall inside of my heart. They seemed to melt all the anger, resentment, and sorrow inside of me. That day, I forgave my father and also repented to God for all the sin that I had committed in my heart over the years. From that day on, a sort of strength was restored in my heart and the resentment and anger inside of me completely disappeared. And more than anything else, my love for my father was restored.

Many people misunderstand God's ministry of *inner healing*. They say that inner healing is a human-centered psychotherapy that comforts rather than removing human sinfulness and brokenness. But that is a misunderstanding. Inner healing is the Holy Spirit's work of bringing to us a spirit of forgiveness and repentance. Only by forgiving the people who have hurt us and repenting of our sins of hatred and enmity, can we be restored in our relationship with both people and God. Unresolved bitter roots of the past create unhealthy emotions in our daily interactions with family and friends and ultimately make it difficult to build an intimate relationship with God.

> "Make every effort to live in peace with everyone and to be holy; without holiness no one will see the Lord. See to it that no one falls short of the grace of God and that no bitter root grows up to cause trouble and defile many."
> (Hebrews 12:14–15)

Inner healing can never replace the Gospel. The only Gospel is Jesus Christ. But Matthew 13 points out to the Christian believer that if God's Word is sown in a field that has been thoroughly cultivated, it bears a bountiful harvest of a 100-, 60-, or 30-fold what was sown.

No matter how good of a sermon we listen to, how often we read the Bible, or how often we attend church services, if the field of our hearts is not cultivated, the Word of God cannot bring transformation to our lives. Even if a farmer sows the best seeds, an uncultivated field cannot absorb the seeds to create a plentiful harvest. Therefore, what a wise field owner does first is to plow his field.

After cultivating the field of my heart by forgiving my father, I enjoyed restoration not only in my relationship with my father but also in my relationship with God. To me, my father had always been a busy and absent person in my life. So, God, who is my spiritual Father, had always seemed to be the same. God, who has a big vision and a lot of work to do, always seemed to be busy. And to be used by God, it seemed like I had to be perfect in everything.

However, after cleaning the field of my heart, I began to see that my spiritual Father, Father God, was different from my physical father. A few days after my reconciliation with my father, God spoke to me as I was praying.

"Mary."

"Yes?"

"You are more important to me than any dream."

(…)

"Even if you don't achieve my dreams, you are special to me just for who you are. Your existence alone is why I love you."

The moment God spoke to me, uncontrollable tears poured down my cheeks. Hearing His words of love, I experienced, for the first time, a love that was so deep and vast that I could not possibly contain or endure the greatness of it. It is this love that began in me a personal, intimate relationship with God, as a *Father*, and a love that is not only continuing but also growing anew every day.

God always tells us that *He loves us*. But why can't we hear His voice? This is not because God's voice is too small or we are lacking in our effort to hear. Rather, it is because of the wounds of the past that prevent us from enjoying healthy relationships with not only people but also God.

But when we cultivate our heart, we begin to see, hear, and feel God's love like we have never before. There is a change in depth when we read God's Word, as we begin to discover how every word in the Bible is like honey, sweet with God's love. Furthermore, there is a change in the way we look at God. Though God is powerful and majestic, we realize, too, that God sympathizes with us and responds to our smallest groans. The reason for my confidence in saying this is because I, too, experienced this.

Through the reconciliation and restoration that I experienced with my father, I was able to resolve my misunderstandings of who God was and, in the end, came to love God more than my life. If anyone can see God's love properly, we cannot help but devote our entire life to Him.

In the beginning, when God created man, He gave mankind innate mental health. In the Garden of Eden, Adam and Eve were in perfect union with God, hearing and responding to His voice. However, by eating from the Tree of the Knowledge of Good and Evil, mankind disobeyed God, breaking the perfect union with Him, and began to live a life of independent will. This independent will is one that refuses the protection, guidance, and perfect will of God. It is a spirit of orphanhood that endeavors to solve one's fears with one's ability yet utterly fails to do so.

We need to hear the voice of God. The words of man are temporary, but the voice of God endures forever. It is God's voice that gives mankind the perfect strength to overcome all things. Above all else, it is God's voice that we need to recover in our lives.

> "The grass withers and the flowers fall, but the word of our God endures forever."
>
> (Isaiah 40:8)

From today on, we need to give our attention to cleaning the fields of our hearts. God is willing to help us become of good soil, a good heart that loves and keeps His Word, bearing fruit of a 100-, 60-, or 30-fold what was sown. When we remove the false self-image, bitter roots, and worldly values inside of us and, instead, become filled with God's Word, powerful breakthroughs will occur in our lives and surroundings.

Chapter 17
Mary's Dream

The more we become of good soil, the clearer God's vision for our life becomes.

When I was in the sixth grade of middle school, my dream was simply to become a global businesswoman. But over the years of my constant relationship with God, God has expanded this dream into greater detail. Now, at age 24, God has given me three dreams: a preacher of God's Word, a global female CEO, and a national leader.

• My First Dream, A Global Preacher of God's Word

Of all places, it is the pulpit where I feel the most joy. As a young child, I remember sitting down with my dolls, muttering to myself for hours as I read books to the imaginary Teddy, Sally, Katie, and Jack. This was my favorite childhood game. As a middle schooler, I found the most fun in helping my friends to study, and as a high schooler, I found the most joy in tutoring my classmates after school. Even as a college student, I found myself not only teaching as a student tutor at the university but also leading Bible study at church, during which time, God began to develop the gift of teaching in me exponentially.

My MBTI personality type is ENFJ, the *Teacher*. The ENFJ personality type feels the greatest satisfaction and happiness when, through their teaching and guidance, others are able to go above and beyond. This personality, which God has given me as a gift to serve others, shines most when I teach God's Word. With parents who are both ministers, I have come to share the same passion for preaching.

With regards to the ministry of preaching, I have four powerful role-models. My first role model is Pastor Billy Yang, my father. Like Pastor Billy, who evangelizes every day with a vision of planting 8,000 churches and imparting 100,000 missionaries, I, too, want to become a global evangelist for world missions. My second role model is Pastor Sharon Yang, my mother. Pastor Sharon has a gift for cultivating people through her preaching and discipleship program. Like her, I want to free the spiritually bound and heal the spiritually broken. My third role model is Pastor Jun Kwang-hoon, my father-in-law. With a vision of achieving the unification of North and South Korea under the Gospel, Pastor Jun has trained more than 100,000 pastors over his entire preaching career. Like Pastor Jun, I want to educate and disciple the next generation of preachers for Korea and the world. Finally, my fourth role model is Pastor Jentezen Franklin of Free Chapel Church located in Georgia, USA. With gifts of praise and playing the saxophone in the Holy Spirit, Pastor Jentezen leads worship in both preaching and praise, during which I strongly feel the presence of the Holy Spirit. Like Pastor Jentezen, who reminds me much of David in the Bible, I want to become a pastor of Spirit-led worship.

As a preacher of God's Word, I dream of worshiping with endless crowds of people at the World Christianity Center, which is to be built under the leadership of Pastor Jun in the next few years. With pastors, missionaries, businessmen, politicians, teachers, and all Christian believers from across the globe, I envision regularly hosting worldwide Holy Spirit movements. It is my absolute, lifelong desire to live as a worshiper who testifies to the world of the beauty and majesty of our living God.

"One thing I ask from the LORD, this only do I seek: that I may dwell in the house of the LORD all the days of my life, to gaze on the beauty of the LORD and to seek him in his temple."

(Psalm 27:4)

• My Second Dream, A Global Female CEO

During my elementary school years living in America, I had no understanding of the concept of *money*. But the moment our family moved to Korea, I understood, instantly. Having lived in a spacious, two-story house in America, I was shocked at the two-room apartment that we moved into when I arrived in Korea. As old as it could possibly be, the walls were covered with holes, and the bathroom water pipes would shoot brown, rusty water when the hot tap was turned on during the winter. But even this shabby apartment we found difficult to afford, and every couple of months, the security guard would come banging on our door to warn us of overdue maintenance fees. It was in these circumstances that I learned what *being poor* meant.

To me, being poor meant not only living in a shabby, small apartment but also having no dream or future. When we moved to Korea in the summer of 2009, my parents could not afford to send me to an international school and had no choice but to register me in a public middle school. For someone who had been born and raised in America her entire life, speaking only Korean for all my class subjects was bound to make me fall behind my peers. With just two months before a nightmare-like enrollment in the local middle school, my mother sent me to a Bible camp. There, though having expected no miracle in my life, I ended up fervently experiencing the greatest miracle—the love of Jesus Christ, for the first time, and the gift of praying in tongues.

One day, a few weeks after returning from the Bible camp, God came and spoke to me while I was praying.

"Mary."

"Yes?"

"Can you give me everything you have?"

"Everything?"

"Yes, trust me."

Though God had not specifically said what *everything* meant, I knew exactly what God was asking for. This was the work of the Holy Spirit who helped me realize God's heart. That night, I pulled out a small box in the deep corner of my closet. In the box was about US$ 1,000 that

I had saved up for five years, ever since the first grade of elementary school. It was *everything* that I had. To give what I could not let go of the most was not easy. But the Holy Spirit gave me courage and faith that God had a plan for my life. Carefully, I arranged the bills to face the same direction and neatly stacked them into the offering envelope that I had brought from church that evening. Sealing the envelope, I wrote on the front with a black pen.

"God, thank you for everything. I love you."

Just two weeks after I gave everything I had to God, someone called my parents on the phone, saying that they wanted to financially support me in attending the most prestigious international school in South Korea for all seven years of middle and high school. Through my obedience, God gifted me an unforgettable experience of His greatness—an experience that remains one of the most powerful testimonies of my life!

In just one month, my parents and I finished the registration and enrollment process, and in mid-August, school began. I loved everything about the school. The school used English, which was my native language, and my teachers and friends were extremely friendly. But little did I know, in what seemed like a dream come true, that God had planned the next seven years to mold and shape me into pure gold.

> "But he knows the way that I take; when he has tested me, I will come forth as gold."
> (Job 23:10)

The school that I attended was the oldest and, therefore, most prestigious international school in South

Korea. Tuition for a year at the school was equivalent to the annual salary of a typical office worker. That is why most of the kids at school were the children of CEOs, celebrities, lawyers, doctors, and professors. As an anecdote, on the first day of school, I became friends with a boy in my class. Playing Rock Paper Scissors while waiting in line for lunch, I gave him a noogie for losing, only to find out that he was the grandson of the owner of the 63 Building, which back then was the tallest skyscraper in Seoul.

Being surrounded by friends of incomparable wealth and status was not an easy thing for me. Giving their friends five-dollar ice-cream cups, which they would buy with their parents' credit cards, skipping afterschool classes at hagwons that cost more than US$ 5,000 a month just because they felt tired, and getting picked up by their private drivers in black sedans, the lives of these kids were completely different from mine. The more I saw them, the more it made me miserable about my circumstances. Living in a two-room apartment, having to shower with cold water in the winter, and being picked up not by a black sedan but a church van covered with

"I love Jesus" stickers, I felt embarrassed. It was then that I determined for myself that I needed to change my dream. I needed to change my dream from becoming a teacher to becoming something that would make the most money in the world. Back then, the person whom I had labeled in my mind as making the most money was the church deacon who had called my parents to offer to financially support me in my studies. To me, this man was rich enough to become my role model, and it was on that day that my dream of becoming a teacher changed to becoming a CEO.

Although this dream was exactly what God had planned for me all along, what God had to do was to first remove my worldly values. The process of God fully weeding out the values of the world inside of me lasted seven years—which were certainly not easy years. I cried out and complained to God, demanding from Him an answer to if there was any blessing in being a pastor's child. But regardless of my rants and cries, God always found a way to bring me back to a place of worship. And in this time of worship, God always made the same request—to give to Him everything I had.

> "For where your treasure is, there your heart will be also."
> (Matthew 6:21)

In the end, what completely freed me from the stronghold of money was the offerings that I gave to God. After I gave God US$ 1,000 in the sixth grade of middle school, I experienced a miracle of reaping an annual tuition of US$ 30,000, which was 30 times what I had sown, for each of the seven years of middle and high school. Giving to God what I loved more than Him ultimately helped me to get rid of the idolatry of money inside of me and changed my attitude toward money. Not only Sunday service and tithe offerings but also offerings to whatever or whomever God touched my heart to serve, I gave and gave.

After the seven years of middle and high school, God touched my heart, now as a high schooler facing enrollment in college, to once again sow everything that I had. Though financially incapable of even applying to college, I had in me a faith that God had built over the years of obedience, and so I obeyed. With faith and gladness, I sowed everything that I had saved over the years to God. And in the fall of that year, God gifted me the miracle of enrolling in Emory University with a full scholarship and financial aid package. At that time, the alabaster jar that I broke was only US$ 1,000, but God, once again, provided for me an annual tuition of US$ 70,000, seventyfold what I had given to Him, for each of the four years. When I gave everything to God, God gave His everything to me. For the four years of college, God poured out an unthinkable sum of US$ 300,000. What a God we serve!

Through these steps of obedience that God required and that I subsequently obeyed, I came to realize what type of God I served and how faithful His guiding hands were. Through the years, I came to know God, not relying on the words of man but personally experiencing, feeling, and hearing from God Himself.

"My ears had heard of you but now my eyes have seen you."
(Job 42:5)

The first thing that I learned throughout the seven years of middle and high school was that God is *not poor*. God is the Creator God Who created the entire universe and is the LORD of all things. Second, God, no matter how rich He is, cannot give His everything to those who are enslaved to money. Why is this? In God's financial system, there is always a *purpose* for money. God's purpose for all finances, from the billions to the single penny, is to *save souls*. That is why, before giving financial blessings to His children, God looks for wise stewards who can manage His money in accordance with His will. To those stewards who are free from the worship of money and worldly values and can solely follow the Word of God, God pours out His money unprecedentedly. I pray that these stewards can be me and you.

> "The Lord answered, 'Who then is the faithful and wise manager, whom the master puts in charge of his servants to give them their food allowance at the proper time? It will be good for that servant whom the master finds doing so when he returns. Truly I tell you, he will put him in charge of all his possessions.'"
>
> (Luke 12:42-44)

After seven years of training in obedience, God restored my dream of becoming a global businesswoman in education and culture. Ever since I was young, God not only allowed me to learn many things but also developed in me giftings through a church-centered life. Learning the violin, piano, guitar, drums, figure skating, ballet, jazz dance, swimming, Chinese, French, and Arabic, I began to experience an exponential growth in these giftings as I served in the church.

It was in the church, when I offered these gifts to God's work, that they began to explode. The first time that I began to accompany on the piano was when the church accompanist repeatedly missed service without notice during my seventh grade of middle school. From then on, God began to provide a place for me to serve in the church. From piano accompaniment to even washing the dishes, I began to serve. Although the eyes of man are limited, the eyes of God do not miss a single thing. All the time and energy that I dedicated to God, God saw. And in just a year, God upgraded my poor piano skills to the same level of the main accompanist and my violin playing, which my mother jokingly regarded as "noise" not "music," to that of a lead violinist at school. And remembering the number of dishes washed and floors mopped, God blessed me with good health ever since. Nothing goes unnoticed in God's eyes.

Being born, raised, and nurtured in the presence of God ever since I was young, I have learned from God the ways in which the Kingdom of God is manifested on this earth. God's Kingdom is built on this earth when people become *worshipers*. It is this vision of raising up worshipers that God has given me. It is this vision of teaching the Word of God in all spheres and industries to free the imprisoned and heal the brokenhearted. It is this vision of bringing those who only tread on the Outer Court to go beyond a mere religious practice to experience the full presence of God in the Holy of

Holies. I want to teach young men and women how to lead a powerful life of worship, both in the church and in their fields of expertise.

So, as a businesswoman of God, I want to begin by building a school that cultivates the spirituality of the younger generation. As I will explain in detail, this school will not only be a learning institution of common academic courses, but also a spiritual institution where students can discover and develop their gifts and talents. It will be a school that increases not only academic knowledge but also the *spiritual volume* of these children. Children will find joy and satisfaction through the discovery of their talents and God-given dreams, and with this, they will overcome the temptations of each generation. Children will long for greater giftings and for such spiritual anointing and be thoroughly trained as worshipers of God. Children will personally encounter the love of God in worship, and according to the gifts that God has given to each person, will become worshipers in all spheres of the outside world, not just in the church. This generation, far transcending ours, will rise up to be a mighty army that represents the living God to all nations and peoples.

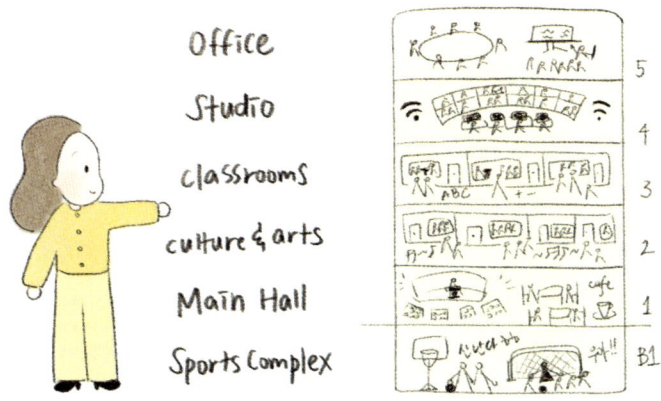

"Your troops will be willing on your day of battle. Arrayed in holy splendor, your young men will come to you like dew from the morning's womb."

(Psalm 110:3)

This illustration is the blueprint for the school that I dream of. This school will be in the form of an afterschool academy that will be open to both believers and non-believers. The sports complex as well as the academic and cultural courses will become extremely popular even to the non-believing youth. As these young adolescents register to play sports or attend typical courses, they will gradually begin to respond to the spiritual atmosphere of the believing staff and peers. For children who are oppressed and bound, engagement in Christian cultural activities, like dancing and performing musicals, will open their hearts. Every morning and evening, worship will be held in the main sanctuary. Throughout the day, the school will also bustle with seminars, meetings, and various conferences with global leaders of the older generations. Finally, the school will go further to not only impact the lives of students but also the lives of teachers. By providing a strong financial infrastructure, the school will protect the faith of Christian teachers who typically slip into the culture of the world due to financial hardships. The school will train and financially provide for gifted teachers, allowing them to wholly commit their God-given talents to His work.

God has a beautiful dream for each and every life. But to achieve such dreams, what each life needs first is *healing*. This is the school's most important goal. Through the Gospel of Jesus Christ, the school will heal the wounds and scars of children with prophetic gifts and go further to anoint them to a life of apostolic calling. Through worship, children will restore their self-image as *children of God* and will receive the gifts of the Holy Spirit to confidently soar like eagles. Sometimes, they may shake and fall, but all teachers and staff of the school will build them up with the love of Christ. As when a mother eagle dives to pick up the falling baby eagle, the school will practice the faithful love of God. Over time, these students will become people of the Holy Spirit, spreading their wings and focusing only on the work of the Holy Spirit. This school will spread nationwide at an unprecedented speed and will stand as an institution that will contribute the most to cultural unification when North and South Korea are reunified. The school will also serve as a key missionary center in the *Back to Jerusalem* movement. All such dreams are not of my personal wisdom and drive but of God's.

> "This is what the Sovereign LORD says: 'See, I will beckon to the nations, I will lift up my banner to the peoples; they will bring your sons in their arms and carry your daughters on their hips.'"
> (Isaiah 49:22)

• My Third Dream, A National Leader

Every summer vacation during my elementary school years, my mother flew with me to Korea to spend the summer at our grandmother's place. This was something that my mother had always done, regardless of our tight financial budget, in order to expose me to my mother country and tongue. During the summer vacation of my third grade of elementary school, while my mother and I were on the subway, we came across an old man who was slightly tipsy from an afternoon's sipping of alcohol. Sitting next to me on the subway, the old man suddenly spoke to my mother.

"Raise this child well, I tell you. She needs to speak Korean well. This kid is going to save the country one day."

Though this old man was slightly intoxicated, my mother recalls that she always kept his words in mind, just like Jacob had kept the dream of his son Joseph in his heart.

God has a good purpose for every individual's life. So, when we deviate from God's will, He continues His faithfulness by redirecting our steps back to align with His will. This is pure grace.

> "His brothers were jealous of him, but his father kept the matter in mind."
>
> (Genesis 37:11)

By the time I graduated from college, I had already planned the course of my life. After getting a job at an American marketing company, I planned to work during the day and attend seminary school courses in the evening. But nothing went as I had planned. Because my will was not what God had planned for me, God shut all the doors that I had envisioned and directed my path elsewhere. This was a path that I had never imagined or prayed for in my entire life. This path took me to the National Assembly Building of Seoul, South Korea.

Upon returning to Korea after graduating from college, I found my father leading prayer meetings in front of the National Assembly building every Wednesday and Saturday. Seeing my father and members of the congregation pray for hours under the scorching sun, I, as the pastor's child, felt uncomfortable not attending. So, in May of 2020, a week after my return to Korea for the summer, I headed over to the National Assembly Building. To clarify, it was not *inside* but *outside* the National Assembly Building that we gathered, looking like a group of nomads. When the prayer meeting started, I realized how difficult a commitment this was. With hissing, poorly equipped microphones, I was led to translate the sermons of the many pastors who attended. Some people, passing by in their cars, would point their middle fingers out the windows, and others would honk their horns in disapproval.

Disturbed about and exhausted from everything that had happened in the span of several hours, I decided, on my first day at the prayer meeting, that this was to be my last day. With such determination, I raised my hands toward the National Assembly Building for the last unison prayer that signified the end of the meeting. Everyone raised their hands up to the sky and began to pray in a loud voice. I, too, raised my hands and called on the name that I loved most, *God*. It was at that moment that God began to speak clearly in my heart. Drawing my gaze to the vast blue sky above the National Assembly Building, He spoke softly but with much clarity.

"Mary, look at the sky. Isn't it so beautiful? I love this land so much. This is a land of the Gospel where countless people have shed their blood, sweat, and tears as they were martyred for my Name. This land is the vision carrier of world missions and the nation of priesthood that I have chosen to prepare for the Second Coming of My Son. But Mary ⋯ My heart is aching."

As if one can do anything for the person whom one loves most, the voice of God that came to me that day completely changed me. The same person who had made a resolution never to attend another prayer meeting ended up being the same person who, through the rain and shine, kept her place in front of the National Assembly Building every week for a whole year. And it was in the very same year that I met Pastor Jun and served as his translator for the memorable August 15th Rally in Gwanghwamun Square of Seoul, South Korea, where hundreds of thousands of people gathered. It was during that year that I became a person of the Holy Spirit, confessing that I would even give my life for the sake of the country that God loved, Korea. All this, as I emphasize, began from my love for God.

Only God perfectly knows the steps of our lives. But when we engage in daily fellowship in worship, prayer, and God's Word, God shares with us an understanding of His plans with greater clarity. As an example, below is an excerpt of a prophetic prayer that God illuminated to me through Pastor Per Ivar Winæss of Norway in the summer of 2019.

Many people will come to you and ask for counseling.

Like Deborah, you have received the anointing from God to not only comfort people with wisdom but also to solve spiritual problems.

People will come to you and say, "Wow, I felt the Lord speaking to me through your teaching."

This is called the Nataph anointing.

I pour the anointing of Nataph into your teaching.

Your teaching will have no limits.

It will be a supernatural teaching and will set people free in many ways.

During your teaching, the Holy Spirit will visit to speak to you so that you will teach in ways you had never thought of.

> "In their hearts humans plan their course, but the LORD establishes their steps."
>
> **(Proverbs 16:9)**

God has a *calling* for every individual. The fulfillment of this calling is not for personal gain and ambition but for the salvation work of God. While the whole world trembles in fear over the end times, God's candle of the Holy Spirit is over Korea as He calls us to pray for the unification of the two Koreas under the Gospel. In times like these, we need to deeply meditate and seek God for a revelation of our calling as an individual and as a nation. In times like these, we must resolve to not defile ourselves with the culture and sin of the world. In times like these, when God has called South Korea as a missionary nation to spread the Gospel to North Korea, China, the Islamic regions, and all the way back to Jerusalem, we must resolve to transform ourselves with the renewing of our minds through the Holy Spirit in a life of worship, prayer, and God's Word.

I love my country, South Korea. And in me, there is a holy desire that God has given me to be a national leader who can solve the spiritual problems of people, environments, and countries. As long as there are people who can give their lives to God not in words but through action-led obedience, every nation will be able to fulfill God's will on this earth. As for Korea, God will surely use this beautiful nation as the most powerful center of global missions. This promise rests not with us but with God.

> "For from him and through him and for him are all things. To him be the glory forever! Amen."
> (Romans 11:36)

Chapter 18
Our Family's Dream

What is our family's dream? What is God's vision for my marriage to Enoch?

God's dream for our family is *salvation work*. This is the dream of God, the life of Jesus, and the work of the Holy Spirit. Through the seven major domains of the world—politics, economy, society, culture, education, religion, and family—God continues to fulfill His salvation work. Among the seven mountains, God's purpose for me and Enoch is to follow in the footsteps of our parents to become preachers of God's Word, to serve missionaries and ministers across the globe through business-led missions, and to lead the spirituality of an entire nation as global leaders.

For God's work, we must receive the anointing of the Holy Spirit. That is why from before marriage until now, Enoch and I keep a lifestyle of reading God's Word and praying daily. Furthermore, we apply the worship of God into the respective fields of our life. We forgive those who have hurt us in the past, apologize to those who we may have hurt, obey what our spiritual leaders advise, and listen to what our parents say. When we hear from each other what to improve on, we accept with gladness and make an effort to change. Though none of these are easy, we remember that the greatest priority of the Christian life is to respond to each subject of obedience that the Holy Spirit reveals.

When we respond step by step to the voice of the Holy Spirit, God begins to entrust us with His work. Through obedience to God, Enoch and I, too, have been entrusted with a work of God—the *Enoch and Mary Missions Organization*. Though titled as cofounders, Enoch and I remember that we are only faithful stewards of what is God's for the time that He has entrusted it to us.

When I was born, my father named me *Mary* in hopes that I would become a woman who serves men and women of God, just like the mother of Jesus, Mary. What amazes me is that the moment I married Enoch, God achieved my father's first-ever prayer request for my life.

Founded in 2021 through our marriage, *Enoch and Mary Missions Organization* is a Christian organization that is centered on cultivating the next generation of youth in Korea. Growing up as pastor's children, both Enoch and I acknowledge that we would not exist today without the helping hand of God. We, like any other child, had talents and dreams. But what achieved such things was the people that God sent to us as channels of His faithful provision. Our vision is to create a strong community system to nurture children who cannot achieve their dreams due to difficult family circumstances. Through the *Enoch and Mary Scholarship Society*, children of pastors and missionaries, as well as those of normal backgrounds, will be selected and awarded scholarships. In addition, through required enrollment in particular courses, the scholarship program will not end with mere financial support but go beyond to cultivate each child into the image of God, so they may thereby gain the greatest blessing of a lifetime—a relationship with God.

Inheriting the vision of both our parents, Enoch and I are called to serve the youth of the next generation, to restore every child to the image of God, and to transform them as key-makers in the seven domains of the world, preparing for the Second Coming of Jesus.

This work is not the desire of man, but a dream that God gives to those who obey. We need to remember that no matter how big or small our dreams are, we are just jars of clay that carry the real surpassing power, Jesus, inside of us. Whether you run a large company or a small supermarket, the only reason you shine is because Jesus is residing inside of you as Lord. That is why we must be humble each and every day.

"But we have this treasure in jars of clay to show that this all-surpassing power is from God and not from us."

(2 Corinthians 4:7)

Chapter 19
And Mary's Last Dream

After I married Enoch, I realized that there was one more dream that God had given me. This last dream, neglected by many but deeply valued by God, was to love my life's companion, my husband, with all my heart for the rest of my life.

As children of God, we need to reflect the love of God through our lives.

Through our words and actions, our spouses should feel the love of God. What kind of love is this? It is a love that endures to listen to one's spouse even when feeling wronged. It is a love that does not become angry when one's spouse is irritated but rather seeks God to reveal the spiritual reason behind such irritation. It is a love that encourages one's spouse who is undergoing low self-esteem and says, "God loves you equally regardless of whether you're qualified or not."

We need to learn how to use heavenly language toward our spouses.

"You're a big help to me."

"There's no other husband like you in this world."

"Marrying you was the best decision of my life."

But there are certain types of spouses who naturally, without consciously thinking, use such heavenly language. What kind of people are they? They are people who have a rich experience of God's love. Just as someone who has been regularly complimented can also compliment others, it is someone who has been loved who can also give love to others.

There are many channels of love in our lives, such as the love of our parents, the love of a friend, and the love

of a lover. However, human love can never fully quench a human's longing for acknowledgment, acceptance, and love. The only thing that can completely and perfectly quench this eternal longing is the love of God through Jesus.

"But whoever drinks the water I give them will never thirst. Indeed, the water I give them will become in them a spring

> of water welling up to eternal life."
> (John 4:14)

What God has commissioned us to is not only the work of saving souls but also the work of saving the people who God has placed in our lives, such as our parents, spouse, siblings, and children. Salvation work does not only mean sharing the Gospel of Jesus. Salvation work goes beyond the acceptance of Jesus to reaching a personal relationship with God, experiencing God's love, overcoming sins, and restoring dreams and visions. It is such a powerful redemptive plan that God has placed in each family and household, and it is such people, who practice the love and faith required for God's redemptive work, who Jesus calls His true disciples.

> "By this everyone will know that you are my disciples, if you love one another."
> (John 13:35)

Epilogue

Just as we do not build a house without a blueprint, so God did not proceed without a plan when He created the heavens and the earth. If we, as God's creations, proceed to construct a house only after having drawn a blueprint, how much more would the perfect God, the Creator of all mankind, have created this world with a perfect, intricate plan!

Many people mistakenly believe that God's plan began with the moment He created the heavens and the earth. But according to God's Word, even before the creation of the heavens and the earth, God had already not begun *but finished* His perfect plan.

> "For he chose us in him before the creation of the world to be holy and blameless in his sight."
> (Ephesians 1:4)

Those who do not know God can never come to realize the purpose, direction, and ultimate destination of their lives. Such a person lives aimlessly, falling into discouragement and frustration when faced with difficult situations and, in extreme cases, resorting to committing suicide. In this life that we only live once, we must know the God who created us, provides for us, and guides us. God calls us His children and loves us dearly. He has prepared His most perfect and good will for us—even before our existence. It is the fulfillment of His will that will bring the greatest satisfaction, happiness, and joy to our lives.

This is the same with marriage.

Getting married in a single month at age 24 to someone

whom I had never met, falling in love with a former high school football player, and meeting my parents-in-law who have become strong pillars of the ministry that I always dreamed of as a young kid, none of it deviated from God's perfect plan.

Sometimes, God's plan may look different from what we expected. Nevertheless, we can trust God's plan not because the path that God shows us looks nice but because it is *God* who is leading the way. When we know who God is, we can have trust in Him. And the time during which we build this trust is called *worship*.

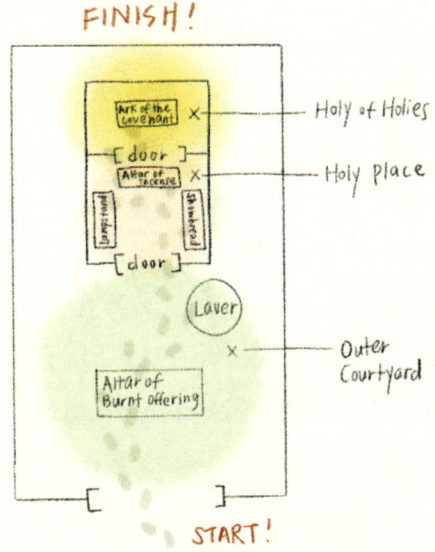

True worship, in which we begin to know God, cut off old sins, and receive dreams and visions, is worship in the *Holy of Holies*. After accepting Jesus as Lord for the first time in our lives, we all start with a so-called *baby faith*, treading and lingering in the Outer Courtyard. Many repent of their sins at the Altar of Burnt Offering and Bronze Laver but continue a self-centered life of worldly values and independent will, repeating the same old sins. But some, among the many, push through in obedience to enter the Holy Place in which they experience the Showbread, Golden Lampstand, and Altar of Incense. This is a life of fellowship with God through the daily reading of God's Word, worshiping, and praying. But the unfortunate thing is that among those who enter the Holy Place, only very few make it to the Holy of Holies. We need to remember that God's ultimate destination for us is to enter the Holy of Holies. This is a place where we are closest to God's complete presence, an intimacy with God that makes even the passing by of the hem of His robe a true reality. This is a life that enjoys perfect union with the Triune God, true freedom and powerful gifts, and the accompaniment of hosts of angels. It is in the Holy of Holies where supernatural powers and breakthroughs take place.

Worship that lingers in the Outer Courtyard brings no powerful transformation into our lives. Our worship must not stop until we go beyond the Outer Courtyard, past the Holy Place, to enter the Holy of Holies.

The fact that I, an ordinary kid with no special talent or gift, was able to receive tens of thousands of dollars' worth of education, get married at age 24, and begin to fulfill the dreams and visions of my prayers is all because of worship.

Worship is a time of honest encounter with God. It is not the fake, "I'm all okay" encounter, but the honest "this is who I am" encounter that God desires. Through worship, God meets those who are bound by all sorts of problems. For those who have daily fellowship with God, sadness becomes joy, helplessness becomes passion, and nihilism becomes dreams and visions. More than any other encounter, the encounter we need most is with God.

In his famous short story *What Do Men Live By*, Russian author Leo Tolstoy answers that people live by love. This is a truth about human nature. All human beings hunger for love and look to love for meaning. I, too, had searched for many people to fill this emptiness, but in the end, could not find anyone. But it was only when I had given up that I began to see that the greatest love had already come to me. This love, Who had planned me from the beginning of time and had never left me, was God.

I eagerly hope that *Marriage Story of Mary* becomes not a perfect book but, like my father would always say, a book that pours out God's love. Among the many encounters and relationships that occur over our lifetime, the greatest meeting we will ever have is not with our parents, our husband, or our children but with God. Even before the beginning of time, God planned you, created you, and named you. There is no sin, no person, and no stronghold that can separate His love from you. The love of God calls you today to make a resolution in your journey back to Him. A daily commitment to worshiping, praying, and reading God's Word will powerfully transform all domains of your life. Today, commit to a life of obedience and expect the supernatural work of our living God!

> "For I am convinced that neither death nor life, neither angels nor demons, neither the present nor the future, nor any powers, neither height nor depth, nor anything else in all creation, will be able to separate us from the love of God that is in Christ Jesus our Lord."
>
> (Romans 8:38-39)

This book is the story of God's love that never gave up on us.
This book is the story of God's love that welcomes the prodigal son back home.
This book is the story of God's love that makes us overcomers through Jesus Christ.

This book is *God's Love Story* for you.

Marriage Story of Mary

초판 1쇄 발행	2022년 5월2일
지은이	양메리
등록번호	2014-000295호
등록일	2014년 10월17일
등록된곳	서울시 성북구 화랑로33길 39 2층 20-3호(청마빌딩)
발행처	(주) 퓨리턴퍼블리싱
이메일	contact @puritianpublishing.co.kr
전화번호	070-7432-6248
ISBN	979-11-954869-9-1 03230
책 가격	16,000원

Founded in 2021 with the marriage of Enoch and Mary, *Enoch and Mary Missions Organization* is a Christian organization that is centered on cultivating the next generation of youth in Korea. Growing up as pastor's children, Enoch and Mary acknowledge that they would not exist today without the helping hand of God. Having talents and dreams like any other child, Enoch and Mary realize that what achieved such things was the people that God sent to them as channels of His faithful provision.

The vision of *Enoch and Mary Missions Organization* is to create a strong community system to nurture children who cannot achieve their dreams due to difficult family circumstances. Through the *Enoch and Mary Scholarship Society,* children of pastors and missionaries, as well as those of normal backgrounds, will be selected and awarded scholarships. In addition, through required enrollment in particular courses, the scholarship program will not end with mere financial support but go beyond to cultivate each child into the image of God, so they may thereby gain the greatest blessing of a lifetime—a relationship with God.